God's Diamond In The Rough

Veronica Pryor-Faciane

Published by Veronica Pryor-Faciane, 2019.

Dedication

With Love and Gratefulness Beyond Measure to my husband David Sr. and wonderfully Blessed children David Jr., Christopher, Joshua and Lil Kaylan. I am appreciative and humbled by your continued support, love, and prayers.

Table of Contents

IN LOVING MEMORY...............................PAGE 2

ACKNOWLEDGMENTS.............................PAGE 4

FORWARDS..PAGE 6

IN LOVING MEMORY...............................PAGE 20

INTRODUCTION....................................PAGE 22

POSSIBLE TRIGGER WARNING....................PAGE 26

CHAPTER 1

WHO IS VERONICA TODAY?.............................PAGE 27

CHAPTER 2

BROKEN TRUST ECOLLECTIONS...............PAGE 35

CHAPTER 3

WHEN WILL IT END?.......................................PAGE 44

CHAPTER 4

WHY LORD?..PAGE 53

CHAPTER 5

HAS MY WAY OUT FINALLY COME?............PAGE 59

CHAPTER 6

DOMESTIC VIOLENCE FACTS/SIGNS.........PAGE 67

CHAPTER 7

A VISION OF A CHAMPION.........................PAGE 72

CHAPTER 8

THE ROADMAP TO MY NEW BEGINNING...PAGE 86

I THANK YOU...PAGE 110

FREE GIFT..PAGE 112

ENDING PRAYER...PAGE 114

REFERENCES...PAGE 116

ABOUT THE AUTHOR...............................PAGE 118

DON'T MISS OUT!.......................................PAGE 122

God's Diamond In The Rough
Strategies To Overcome Traumatic Life Experience

———— ⌘ ————

Copyright © 2019 Veronica P. Faciane, MA
Cover Photographer: Ashley Henderson
Tribute to Mom Photographer: Lacrecia Fergurson-Terrance

———— ⌘ ————

ISBN:978-1-5136-4642-8
E-book- ISBN:978-1-5136-4643-5

In Loving Memory

Patricia Ann Davis-Pryor

a/k/a Pat
June 26, 1950 –March 23, 2015

I am dedicating this book in memory of my mother, Patricia Ann Davis Pryor and all people who have died at the hands of their abuser, whether it be by physical death or mental death. Domestic violence has a lasting effect on individuals, even if they are not with the abuser currently. Through my journey, I have learned that there are so many people walking around dead.

By this I mean they are just existing on a day to day basis and not living their best-blessed lives. My mom transitioned (passed away) on March 23, 2015, because of the mental and physical toll that domestic violence had on her life.

She was unable to get out of her mind. She could not rid herself of the dissonance in her mind (an inconsistency between one's attitudes and behaviors) like so many others, due to depression, she stopped eating and transitioned (passed). There are many, who continually, tell themselves stories that are not positively serving them.

I will be her voice from the grave, letting others know that they don't deserve to be beaten, cursed, degraded and torn apart mentally, physically, spiritually and financially. I miss my mom dearly. No one should ever feel, that after being married over 40-plus years or any amount of time, they were never truly loved.

> *Mama, I Love You!*
> **Till We Meet Again**

Acknowledgments

Thank God for His covering and protection along with my life's rough journey. If it were not for His Grace and Mercy, I would not be able to tell you about my life's transformational story. God gave me the desires of my heart by allowing me to meet and marry my King, David Faciane Sr.

He who finds a wife finds what is right and receives favor from the LORD.
~(Proverbs 18:22 ~NIV)

I AM GRATEFUL FOR OUR continued growth along this journey called life, together. With our union, God has blessed us with three handsome, loving and intelligent boys and one very bossy, bright and cute little girl. I am equally blessed to have another son and five beautiful daughters from our blended family along with our grand-children.

THERE ARE SO MANY PEOPLE I am grateful for pouring into my life and imparting the knowledge I needed for my mind to be transformed. To name a few of those who were influential: Rev. Roosevelt Pryer Sr., Gayle Perkins, Shirley Blount, Harold Robinson, in memory of Latecia Walker a/k/a Cookie, Enger Kichen, K. Lopez, N. Washington, Caris L. Reed (a Woman of God who started as my 1st writing accountability partner. I cannot express the gratitude I have for her and the prayers she prayed when I wanted to stop due to the continual adversities of life.), Catherine E, Storing (mentor) Vanessa A. Williams (prayer warrior/Bff), Jay Diamond, Maridonna Burgin, Pastor Debbie Johnson, Twahna P. Harris founder of the Butterfly Society, Valencia Griffin-Wallace of Define U Radio (mentor), Kathy Kidd of Kidd Marketing (mentor), Keri Murphy founder of Inspired Living (mentor), Susie Carder (profit coach/mentor), Lisa Nichols founder of Motivating the Masses (mentor), Bernard Terrace Elementary Family, my church families' Rosehill Baptist Church of Rosedale, La., Fairview Baptist Church and Beacon Light Baptist Church of Baton Rouge, La. Also, last but certainly not least my four siblings Catrinna (Clarence), Edward Jr. (Muriel), Milton (Darcel), and Timothy. I am Grateful beyond Measure, and I know the Best Is Yet to Come!

Forwards

My Lil Cousin Veronica

When I think about my cousin Veronica, I can go back as far as when she was 4 years old. Her parents were very selective about who watched them. That privilege was not given to many, so; I felt like I must be all right because they allowed me to watch them. I can remember them being so cute and I loved watching them when their parents went out. I loved my family, so I don't even remember getting paid. My relationship with my cousin, her dad, was what I considered as good. I thought he could be loud and hard at times. He commanded respect always! As their family grew, I would have three children to watch. Over time, they seemed to get very quiet. I remember mentioning it to my mom, his mother's sister that they have changed. I told her they seem to be scared for some reason. I told her something is wrong. I didn't know what was wrong until now.

~Cousin Chenell

My Friend Veronica

"I'VE KNOWN VERONICA since 2011, our boys were playing on the same little league team. It's there, when I first saw her dedication as a mom. In time, our relationship grew from team moms to friends. Our connection grew stronger over time; I was able to see her strength and faith as a wife and her dedication to the family institution. As a confidant, she shared with me her testimony of abuse and the struggles that she was still dealing with, but she was determined not to allow her past to win. In many conversations, Veronica shared how she wanted to take what almost broke her and used it to put the pieces of others back together. She's always lamented about how her story could help someone else deal with and overcome the fear and shame of being abused. Through all her shattered pieces, Veronica was able to love her family still, be a supportive friend, be a faithful church member and a person of great strength and moral character, all while encouraging others along the way. I read somewhere before that a broken crayon can still color. Her story is one of strength, courage, faith, and determination and it's not finished. She will be able to touch many along her journey. Veronica is truly a gem, and I'm glad to call her my friend."

~Minister Vanessa Williams

My Testimony to a Special Woman, Veronica Faciane

Veronica Faciane and I have been friends for a long time. Before I had the privilege of teaching her three boys' in first grade, I'd pass her in the halls of Bernard Terrace. She made her presence known to everyone and was pretty much a permanent fixture at our school. What I admired about her then and still do to this day, is her caring, loving, and giving nature to everyone with whom she meets.

We became close friends when I began teaching her first born. She adopted my classroom and became "our room mother." She has always had a way about her that makes one feel loved and protected. Like a mother bird watching over her babies, "she just swept us up and took us underneath her wings." Talk about feeling blessed! I knew what it meant for my class when I had one of her children, which was that we were going to be fully taken care of by her generosity of time and money! There was no limit to her helpfulness to the students me. She provided classroom treats, copied students' homework packets, chaperoned field trips and was "Mama" to many a student. Her passion for helping others is endless. One year, she worked in my classroom on her lunch break to assist me in putting together homework material for ALL my classes.

I realize that in one's lifetime, meeting a person like Ms. Faciane is a rare occurrence. Moreover, trust me when I say that I feel our paths have met for a reason. Little did I know at the time, the real testament to our friendship was manifested when she reached out to help me when I wasn't currently teaching one of her children. It was this random act of kindness that touched my life and made a real difference in my life and the decisions I have made.

When my husband died last May, she was instrumental in leading me in the right direction when it came down to making decisions about my future. I was distraught, confused, and lacked confidence. One summer evening, I received a phone call from her, and we talked for a good while. Hearing me go on, she encouraged me to seek counseling, stating that it could help. She shared some of her own stories with me and went on to say how much counseling had helped her and her family. I took her advice, and, I am so grateful to her because it led me on the right path to peace.

Currently, because her children are not attending my school this year, I do not get to see her smiling face every day in person, and I do miss that; however, we do stay in touch through social media, and for that I am thankful. I realize that she has more lives to touch, in different ways, and on different paths. I am confident that whomever Veronica meets, she will be a blessing to them as well. My prayers are that the feelings of peace and love that she bestows onto others will be presented onto her.

~All my love, Sheila Couvillion

Veronica's Nannie

VERONICA'S MOM PATRICIA and I were friends since the 4th grade. We met through one of my cousin's when I moved to New Orleans in 1959. We became friends instantly. We went all the way through high school together. We ended up losing contact with the cousin that introduced us. In my heart, that was the way it was to be. She was only in our lives for a season. In 1967, I dated a young man, and that was how Veronica's mom met her dad. As time went on, we (the young man I dated) broke up, but Pat continued dating her future husband. After graduating from high school in 1969, they remain to date until they married in 1970. In 1971, God blessed them with a beautiful baby girl who became my godchild, Veronica. As the years passed, Veronica's mom and I grew apart, but we kept in touch periodically. My knowledge of Veronica's life as she was growing up and what could have been happening to her never crossed my mind. Through all the years when I saw the family, it appeared as if they were, One Big Happy Family!

I REMEMBER WHEN VERONICA was hospitalized, I think it was 2002. Her mom called me to tell me that Veronica was in the hospital, but not once did she ever say that Veronica tried to take her life. I can't remember what the reason was that she explained to me, but it wasn't about her trying to commit suicide. The truth came out to me after Veronica, and her husband were married. After their honeymoon, Veronica called me and asked if she and her husband could visit. She stated she wanted to talk to me about something. When they arrived at my home, she burst into tears.

She and I went into another room, and she began to tell me what happened. Her father was sexually molesting her and her sister. I asked her, what are you saying to me? I could not believe what she was saying. At that moment, I began to cry. I was her other mother, and I felt helpless. All I could tell her was to pray. I knew in my mind that something else had to be done. Her mother did not say anything, so I did not either.

VERONICA WOULD CALL me crying, and I felt helpless and powerless. I felt a mother should always protect her children. My godchild was reaching out to me, and I didn't help. I prayed many nights, asking God to give me the strength, to help keep her stable, and she never knew that I was falling apart, with my demons. I kept praying. Through another incident happening and by the grace of God, my prayers were answered.

I BELIEVE GOD ALLOWED this to manifest again so that things will be revealed and her father is arrested. Her mom became sick, and I don't think she realized how much of a victim she was. In the months and years that followed, Veronica's mom stopped eating. I went to visit her in the hospital. She had stopped doing everything. Her body was shutting down, right before all of us. Months later, she passed away. Veronica tried helping her mom all that she could. After all that had happened to her, she loved her mom with unconditional love.

I am so grateful to God that through his love, His grace, and His mercy He kept Veronica. Her test became her testimony. No one should have to go through what she and her sister went through. By the grace of God, she has turned her test into her glory. Because now, she can tell her story. Much Love Sweetheart. I am so proud of you. I know mama is smiling. My friend was a victim of abuse. I think she was tired of fighting, and she felt the best thing was for her to close her eyes and allow God to take her home. I miss my friend so much! She is a constant reminder that mental, sexual, physical, and emotional abuse is real.

~Shirley Blount

Veronica's Children

MY MOM WAKES UP EARLY now, feeds us and works hard every day. My mom before did not eat or do much at home for a long time. It made me feel very sad, and her family members kept dying making her more depressed. She started telling her coworkers and some family members how sad she was. My mom started feeling better after she started moving more. My mom loves things more now, and she takes care of us. My father had to do so much because of my mother being sad, and I am so grateful for my dad. Now, my mom and dad are the best.

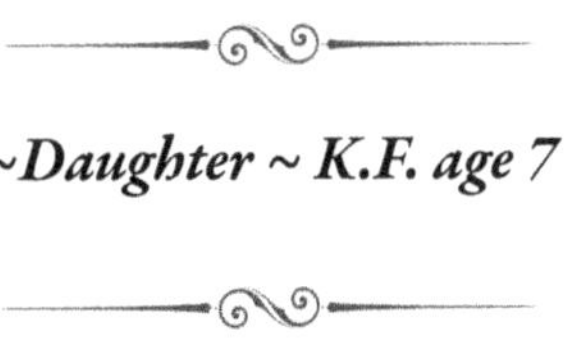

~Daughter ~ K.F. age 7

AT FIRST, MY MOM SHE would not eat. She would sleep over the weekend and would not get out of her bed. I did not understand how and why she did that. I remember going to her room, when my dad went to the store, to see if she was dead. Daddy would tell us to not go in the room, but I had to see my mom. I love her and I felt she did not know we were alive sometime. How could she sleep for so long? Now, she is the best mom ever because she is fun. Don't get me wrong, I am 10, and she can be mean when I want to have my way.

~Son ~J.F Age 10

I HATED SEEING MY MOM depressed! She would never eat, drink or talk to us for a long time. My dad was the one who took care of us because my mom did not get out of bed. I was sad and confused. It was hard for my mind to be in my school work. Now, I see greatness in my mom. She has started speaking more and going out telling others about her past. The new changes I see in my mom makes me so happy and

grateful. I am starting to talk more too!

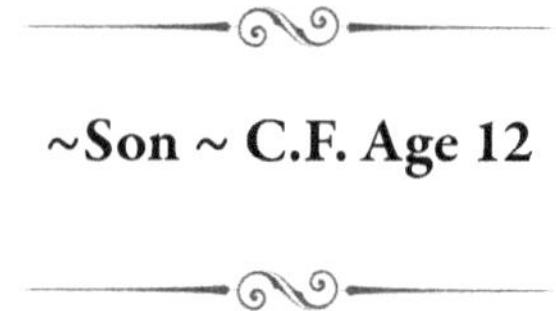

~Son ~ C.F. Age 12

ON FRIDAYS, I WOULD try to talk to my mom as much as possible, because once nighttime came, I knew I would not see her until Monday in the evening. She never moved fast in the morning. So, my dad would be taking care of us. He would try to wake her up to eat, and she didn't. That would scare me so much. I remember sitting by the door hoping she would come out. When my dad would be washing or go outside, I would sneak into the room and sit there.

MY MOM LOOKED LIKE someone put a spell on her. I thought she was dead. I have focus issues and thinking about my mom did not help. I had so many thoughts going through my mind during this time that I had problems focusing. On top of all of that, being teased about my size all the time at school by students and have adults constantly compare me to my middle brother who was taller, was irritating. I felt like I didn't care over time about anything. I guess you could say I was becoming depressed too. I would not eat at school because my appetite was not there.

NOW LIFE IS AMAZING! No, I am not taller than my brother, but my mom is there to help me with my mindset. I had a teacher say, "do not pick him for a sporting event," due to my size. I was able to discuss it with my mom. I know teachers are not perfect, but they should be mindful of the lives placed in their care. I am aware their job is stressful, but we experience stress too.

We are now a family, a team! I have my dad and mom, the person that I can confide in, and she makes everything feel ok. I am very grateful and super blessed!

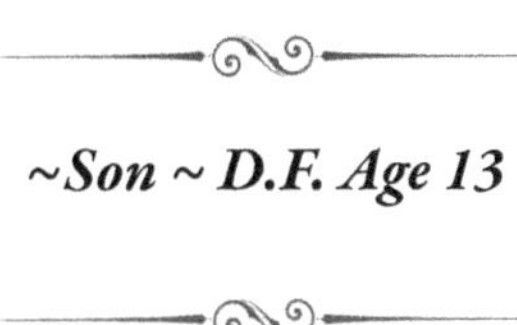

~Son ~ D.F. Age 13

A Confidant

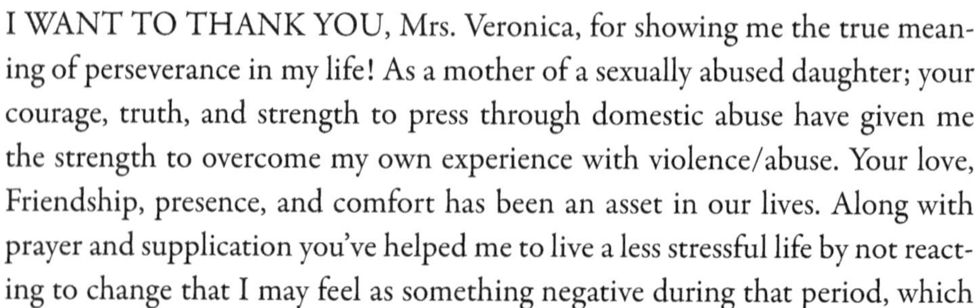

I WANT TO THANK YOU, Mrs. Veronica, for showing me the true meaning of perseverance in my life! As a mother of a sexually abused daughter; your courage, truth, and strength to press through domestic abuse have given me the strength to overcome my own experience with violence/abuse. Your love, Friendship, presence, and comfort has been an asset in our lives. Along with prayer and supplication you've helped me to live a less stressful life by not reacting to change that I may feel as something negative during that period, which often transcends into something victorious later with patience and a change in my point of view. Again, thank you for your admirations and inspirations in overcoming sexual abuse within our family.

~T. Sanders

A Friend & Mother Figure

I MET THIS WONDERFUL, warmhearted, genuine person named Veronica Pryor-Faciane years ago. From the start, we built an awesome relationship. She is always positive and sincere with everyone she meets. I can call her early in the morning or late at night, to talk, and she will make the time to be my motivation and light for transformation. I love this Woman of God and her entire family. Thanks for being a friend, mother figure and inspiration to me.

Xoxo
~Leshonda Lindo

My Wife

WHERE DO I BEGIN ABOUT this woman I love? Well when I first laid eyes on her, I felt like I was in a dream. It reminded me of what my mother told me, "Son, you will know your soul mate because you will feel like she was a gift sent from Heaven." When I looked at her, I knew she was the one. She came looking for her father. I had a hosepipe washing a truck, and I was wondering why she and her mom were staring at me. Well, when I snapped out of it, I realized I was wetting my feet and not the truck (lol). I went to go and get her father to them. From that moment on she became my soul mate.

TIME PASSED THROUGH the good, bad, and the ugly we have stayed together. I remember her, telling me, on our wedding day, she needed to talk to me. I was just happy to be her husband, and I had no clue what she was about to say. I was excited that one of my dreams came true of being a married man. When she started talking, she told me about the 30 years of abuse she experienced from her father. I was speechless and blown out of the water with what she expressed. I had an idea something was not right, but not this. I was mad at myself because I did not get her out there earlier. How could he do this to his daughter? I have daughters,' and it made me sick to my stomach.

WHEN SHE EXPRESSED to me about her father, she told me that if I did not want to stay married, I could have the marriage annulled. I looked at her like she was crazy. I said to her that I loved her, I wasn't going anywhere, and we would get through this together. From that day forward, we have stayed together for almost 17 years for the good, bad and the ugly. Many times, I questioned God, but I remembered my promise to my mother. My mom told me I was a strong man and no matter what to hang in there. I did just that!

IT WAS NOT EASY, AND I was determined to show her I was not going to hurt or give up on her. My baby jumped and fought in her sleep. I felt so sorry for her and all that she has experienced. When a man loves a woman is all I can say. I am so proud of the fantastic, unique, beautiful and remarkably awesome transformation I see in her. Thank God Daily for my soul mate, my best friend and my lovely wife. God has blessed me with four more beautiful children in my later years through our union. She was determined to get it together, and she did.

My Queen, I Will Always Love You,
~David a/k/a "Duke"

My Big Sis from the Other Mother

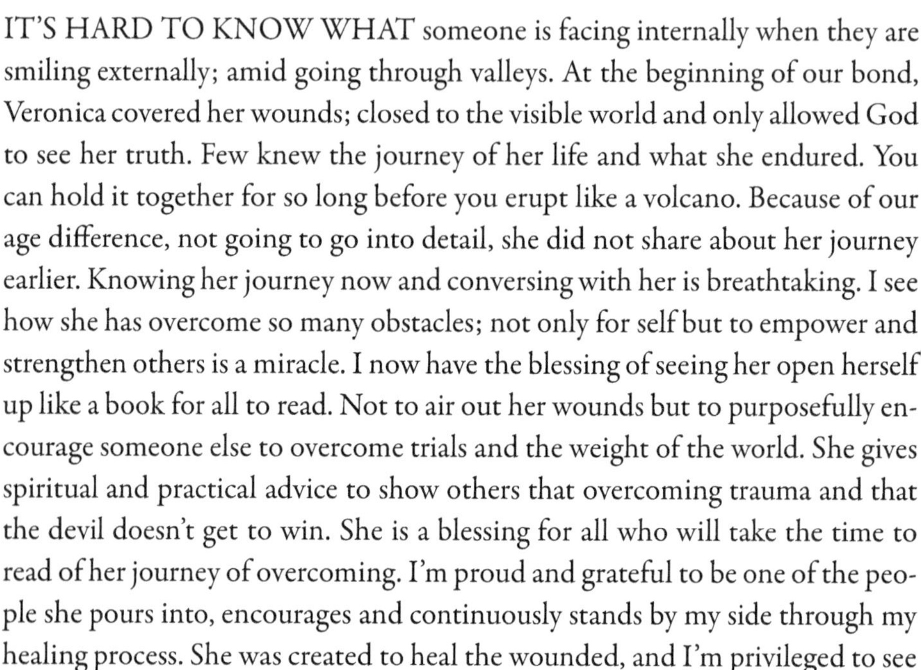

IT'S HARD TO KNOW WHAT someone is facing internally when they are smiling externally; amid going through valleys. At the beginning of our bond, Veronica covered her wounds; closed to the visible world and only allowed God to see her truth. Few knew the journey of her life and what she endured. You can hold it together for so long before you erupt like a volcano. Because of our age difference, not going to go into detail, she did not share about her journey earlier. Knowing her journey now and conversing with her is breathtaking. I see how she has overcome so many obstacles; not only for self but to empower and strengthen others is a miracle. I now have the blessing of seeing her open herself up like a book for all to read. Not to air out her wounds but to purposefully encourage someone else to overcome trials and the weight of the world. She gives spiritual and practical advice to show others that overcoming trauma and that the devil doesn't get to win. She is a blessing for all who will take the time to read of her journey of overcoming. I'm proud and grateful to be one of the people she pours into, encourages and continuously stands by my side through my healing process. She was created to heal the wounded, and I'm privileged to see her walk into her destiny!

~LaToya Walker, spiritual sister, written September 21, 2018

In Loving Memory

~ LaToya R. Walker ~

September 9, 1985 – December 19, 2018

MY SWEET BABY SISTER from another mother and father, transitioned December 19, 2018, after her battle with cancer. She was a powerful, loving, giving person and most of all Woman of God. My heart aches writing this; however, I rejoice for the precious time I was given with her. Toya was in the process of writing her memoir about her life's journey also. We spoke on numerous occasions about the self-publishing process due to her passion for writing. She desired to help others, by living an exemplary life of how to go through life's journey with courage and strength. I watched her ***becoming*** process from a little girl into a ***Queen of Valor***. She never gave away her smile to life's challenges. I Love You.

Till We Meet Again

Introduction

FIRST AND FOREMOST, I want to thank you, yes you, the reader in advance for taking your precious time and opening your heart to reading about my life's journey. It is my hope that each reader can apply the steps utilized along my life's journey for the advancement and cultivation of planting positive seeds for your individual growth towards developing a Positive New Identification (New ID). This is part of my mission in the development of my new business as an author, transformational speaker, and life coach. No longer lingering and living in areas of their lives that are not serving them in a manner that brings joy, peace, balance, happiness, and true self-love.

EVERYONE EXPERIENCES various obstacles, trials, pain, loss, hardships, valley experiences, adversities, afflictions, tribulations and any other words you may choose to express or define the hurt and sorrow that have faced you along your journey thus far. However, the key to living your best or worst life is ***all in your mind***.

Whether You Think You Can, or Think You Can't .....You're Right
~Henry Ford

Happiness is a state of mind. It's just according to the way you look at things.

~Walt Disney

For the mind set on the flesh is death, but the mind set on the spirit is life and peace.
~ (Romans 8:6 ~ NIV)

IT IS MY HOPE THAT you will embark upon a journey of self-discovery, self-transformation, if you choose, learning from my life's experiences of overcoming years of domestic violence and incest suffered at the hands of my birth-father, yes that is right, I did say it was at the hands of my biological father.

And do not be conformed to this world, but be transformed by the renewing of your mind, so that you may prove what the will of God is, that which is good and acceptable and perfect.
~ (Romans 12:2 ~NIV)

ALSO, I WANT TO GIVE you a heads up, that this manuscript has a gamete of emotions flowing throughout my story of domestic violence and incest. This story documents 28 years of sexual (incest), spiritual, mental, verbal, non-verbal and financial abuse by my birth-father, who also was a minister. But God! It is imperative for individuals to have a personal relationship with their maker (which is God for me) or a spiritual belief system. Based on research by the Australian Institute of Family Studies, (2013) the following was noted to put into perspective things experienced along my life's journey and your journey during and after sexual abuse:

"WITHIN THIS DOCUMENT, it was pointed out that the adverse mental health effects after sexual childhood trauma consist of post-traumatic symptoms, depression, substance abuse, helplessness, negative attributions, aggressive behaviors, and conduct problems, eating disorders, anxiety, more recently linked to psychotic disorders (including schizophrenia and delusional disorder) and personality disorders. When children have experienced penetration, they are more at risk for developing psychotic and schizophrenic syndromes.

UPON FURTHER READING, it was noted that more extreme mental health problems relating to suicide ideation, attempts, and actual suicides increase when the perpetrator is affiliated with religious organizations. There was a Victorian Parliamentary Inquiry which documented that 40 Victorian people allegedly abused by Catholic clergy had committed suicide in recent years. When individuals experience sexual victimization from childhood to adulthood, there is a higher probability of suicide attempts and fatal overdoses, among both men and women.

Children that were exposed to sexual abuse involving attempted or completed sexual penetration had rates of mental health disorders, including suicidality, which was 2.4 times higher than those of children not so exposed. It is essential to document that all victims of child sexual abuse develop mental health or adjustment difficulties during their adulthood. However, it is imperative to mention the sleeper effects can manifest via triggers during the later stages of the victim's life by certain life events.

A low percentage was stated within studies on clergy-perpetrated sexual abuse also indicates that boys may be particularly susceptible to abuse of this type and to the effects that play out in adulthood. A large-scale study on abuse allegations in the Catholic Church in the US and a smaller scale study in Australia on allegations against Anglican clergy documented the victims were males. Studies note victims who have experienced trauma by clergy, and other powerful authority figures tend to have particularly devastating effects. This devastation was pointed out by the fact that the families of many victims were active within the work of the church family. The abuse manifested over an expanded period, like many cases of incest; adults tend not to believe the victim when it is brought to the family's attention; which often also occurs within instances of incest. The church leaders usually try to silence victims hoping to avoid scandal. Many of the victims did not disclose the abuse until adulthood, again like in most cases of incest. The trauma of clergy sexual abuse compiled together literature which provided some theoretical foundations notating that this trauma can dramatically alter the trajectory of psychosocial, sexual, and spiritual development. It challenges the victims' trust, sense of self, sexual identity, and social and cognitive development."

MY TRANSFORMATION THROUGH formal therapy is perhaps often unheard of in such a short period, beginning in November 2014, through the present. It is my mission to let others know via my transparency, that I, that you, that we, will no longer have to exist on a day to day basis, but I, that you, that we all are learning to live our best lives. I am continually overcoming the traumas of abuse daily. You too can do the same, Queen or King, (names I use to describe your unequivocal worth), if you decide to say in your heart, 'I am worth true peace which begins with one decision.' If you are just the least bit curious or desire to experience the positive and uplifting transformation that I am undergoing, do continue reading and remember, ***Your Best Is Yet to Come!***

Possible Trigger Warning:

FOR THOSE CURRENTLY suffering domestic violence/incest or survivors of domestic violence/incest: **Please note** the following stories about violence and sexual assault will be extremely strong and descriptive in some cases. Reader, please be mindful of possible damaging emotional responses due to the nature of the forthcoming information. I hope that you will be able to see past my tragic experiences to see how I choose to push into my next and become the Diamond God has intended me as well as you to be no matter what form or type of trauma you experienced.

Chapter 1
Who is Veronica Today?

I am sure many are wondering why I have a desire to tell my story besides being my mom's voice from the grave. I am a very compassionate person and sharing my account allows me to heal as well. This humanistic view gives me hope that someone else can experience the freedom of the mind, body, and soul I have now experienced. Not speaking my truth is non-negotiable. My pain was not experienced in vain. I have always loved doing puzzles and being successful figuring them out. The biggest challenge for me was figuring out how to find peace and balance in my shattered life that is now in the rebuilding process.

NOW, I HAVE A PEACE that surpasses all understanding, and that is golden. I wake up every day with thanksgiving in my heart. Oh, don't think I wake with no challenges with four children (lol). I choose to work with them and my mind on how I perceive my mornings. It is a feeling like no other, seeing the positive in everything no matter how sad or angry a situation may make me. For example, my children get up mad, because they get in each other's way while trying to begin their day. So, either I can get mad and yell along with them, or I can control the situation and not allow the situation to control me. I calmly let them know their expectations. This specific action can leave lasting scars within my children's lives because I was a yeller too. That was the type of environment I grew up in which is very unhealthy. Thus, you repeat what you know, but I choose to grow and change that family trait. Yes, I am bobbing and weaving through life's obstacle course. My mindset shift is key to the smile on my face. It is critical that I keep stress, anxiety, and depression at bay since I desire to live my best and balanced life.

BEING A MOM OF FOUR, a wife, and working a full-time job, I was also a full-time graduate student as of November 2018, Whew…Yessssss!! I am an alumnus of Grand Canyon University, graduating with a 3.41GPA, earning a Master's Degree in Psychology with a Concentration in Life Coaching. In 1994, I graduated from the Xavier University of Louisiana where I was a member of Alpha Kappa Mu Honor Society, and in 1989 I graduated from L.W. Higgins High School where I was on the honor roll also. Despite all the challenges I faced throughout my life, I have always had a determination for greater.

CURRENTLY, I HAVE CHOSEN to start transitioning into a transformational speaker/life coach and author role while continuing to work in my current position as an auditor. Being a parallelprenuer can be very challenging with the number of responsibilities I face daily. Did you notice I chose to utilize the word challenging and not overwhelming? I had to watch what I spoke into my life/universe if I wanted to experience a happy life, feeling free and enjoying every emotion with a new positive perspective. This new positive point of view has changed my life's journey in a peaceful and serene direction. No matter what people say or do, I have balance and joy, unspeakable joy in my life. I laugh when I am approached by the "I remember when crew." We live in a society of people that what to laugh and lay things from your past at your feet. In my opinion, having a mindset of "who cares what you remember…. "Frankly" made my mental life better. I no longer require recognition from someone to affirm me as a worthy individual. (deep breath) that is like a breath of fresh air, no longer needing others approval, feeling true self-love makes me **Grateful Beyond Measure!**

The tongue has the power of life and death, and those who love it will eat its fruit.
~ (Proverbs 18:21-NIV)

MY NEW MINDSET ALLOWS me to view challenges differently, turning those events into a positive learning experience. My current views about life:

- I have changed negative thoughts into positive ones by making lemonade from life's lemons.

- I no longer allow my mind to be in a state that is captivated and encapsulated by stagnate depression, stress, and anxiety. (Freedom, Yes Lord, the darkroom is gone.)

- I am productive despite having challenges with ADHD and domestic violence trauma.

- I am a warrior and not a worrier anymore. I can let go of things and situations I have no control over.

- I am not overwhelmed by the healing process.

- I let go of the "why me?"

- I am the CEO of my life, firing and hiring individuals that do not serve my continual growth.

- I do not live in fear.

- I live to please me and God 1st and foremost, no longer requiring or seeking approval from others to help me define my self-worth.

- I no longer feel obligated when others that I love fail.

- I now see intimacy moments as a positive experience in life.

- I do not allow the opinions of others to define my happiness or decision-making process.

• I feel therapy is just as important as going to a primary care physician.

• I love my body.

• The emotional reactions from the past (nightmares/flashbacks)
are not as frequent.

• I no longer live in fear, shame, guilt (my birth-father's decisions
where not my choices), and humiliation (Others may not understand my old normal, but it is ok.) Transparency and facing my truth
were vital to my healing.

• I choose to foster growth and not self-destructive behaviors within
my marriage, due to old fears of possibly being hurt by a man again.

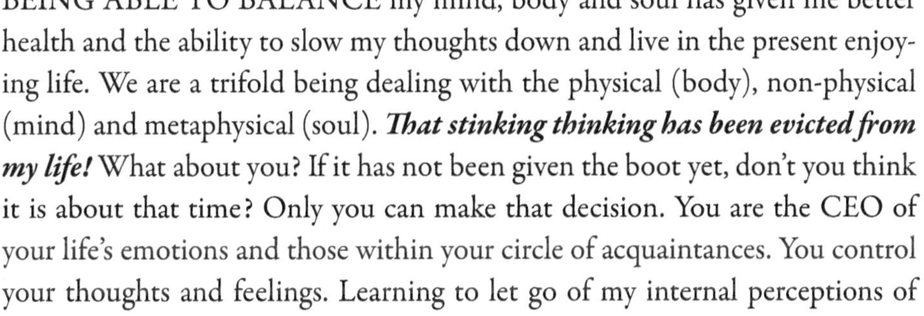

BEING ABLE TO BALANCE my mind, body and soul has given me better
health and the ability to slow my thoughts down and live in the present enjoying life. We are a trifold being dealing with the physical (body), non-physical
(mind) and metaphysical (soul). *That stinking thinking has been evicted from
my life!* What about you? If it has not been given the boot yet, don't you think
it is about that time? Only you can make that decision. You are the CEO of
your life's emotions and those within your circle of acquaintances. You control
your thoughts and feelings. Learning to let go of my internal perceptions of
how I thought others should respond to me interfering with my daily emotions.
Letting go that thought process was vital in me becoming the Queen I Am.

I WILL NOT LET ANYONE walk through my mind with their dirty feet.
~ Mahatma Gandhi

MY DESTINY OF SPEAKING my truth is helping to diminish my depression, stress, and anxiety, focusing on faith and God's promises and not the devil's voice of doubt.

For my thoughts are not your thoughts, neither are our ways my ways," declares the Lord. As the heavens are higher than the earth, so are my ways higher than your ways and my thoughts than your thoughts.
~ (Isaiah 55: 8-9-NIV)

I AM GRATEFUL BEYOND Measure for my new view of life which brings me joy, unspeakable joy, but it has not always been this way. Please understand that the history forthcoming outlines trials that have cleared the path for greater along my life's journey. When I was going through, I thought God hated me. No, I DID! Once I stopped procrastinating with doing the inner mental work and started producing the positive thoughts needed for change, I became a Master Mason, laying a solid foundation towards my greater development I developed the blueprint for my transformation with guidance from God, therapist, mentors and plenty of prayer warriors. The building blocks I selected paved the way for strength not weakness, clearer vision and not a distorted or foggy view. Optimism was cultivated, and pessimism was buried. I will share with you some of the traumatic experiences that occurred throughout my life leading to the present.

OVER TIME, THE FEELING of being dead and having no hope diminished with each new positive decision I made. Each decision helped to pave the way in erasing my stinking thinking. **NO LONGER** will I go through the motions daily of existing, never truly living.

Life's motto: Queen Veronica let things go, so that you can grow, and live in the service of helping others to be better and not bitter.... I forgive daily for my peace.

~Veronica Pryor-Faciane

Life is 10% what happens to us and 90% how we react to it.
~Author unknown

GUESS WHAT? I LEARNED how not to be a people pleaser. Is that you currently? Always making yourself responsible for helping others at the expense of your happiness? I was that person.... Deleted...Yes, it was imperative for me to rid myself of those habits during my transformational process and remove that mindset. Does this sound familiar? Do you sacrifice yourself to please others? Before that, I was a rescuer 24/7. Always desiring to help others, appeared to fulfill the void that I was missing. Don't get me wrong; I love helping people. I do not particularly appreciate seeing anyone suffer, yet, I continued to suffer behind closed doors.

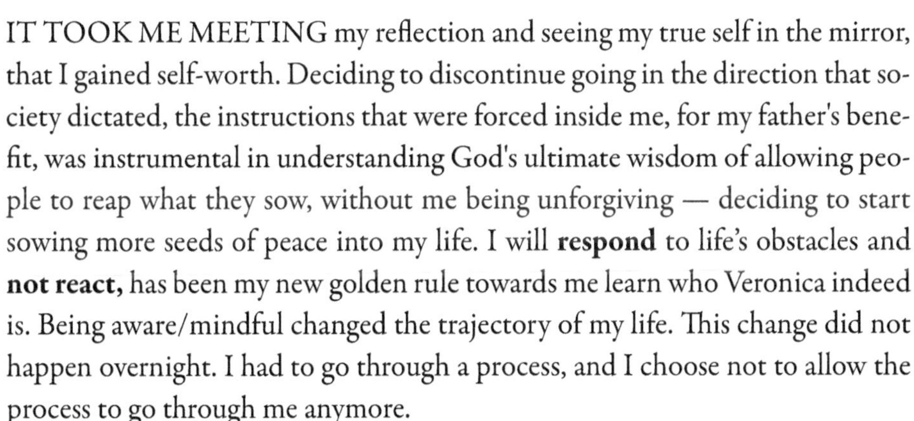

IT TOOK ME MEETING my reflection and seeing my true self in the mirror, that I gained self-worth. Deciding to discontinue going in the direction that society dictated, the instructions that were forced inside me, for my father's benefit, was instrumental in understanding God's ultimate wisdom of allowing people to reap what they sow, without me being unforgiving — deciding to start sowing more seeds of peace into my life. I will **respond** to life's obstacles and **not react,** has been my new golden rule towards me learn who Veronica indeed is. Being aware/mindful changed the trajectory of my life. This change did not happen overnight. I had to go through a process, and I choose not to allow the process to go through me anymore.

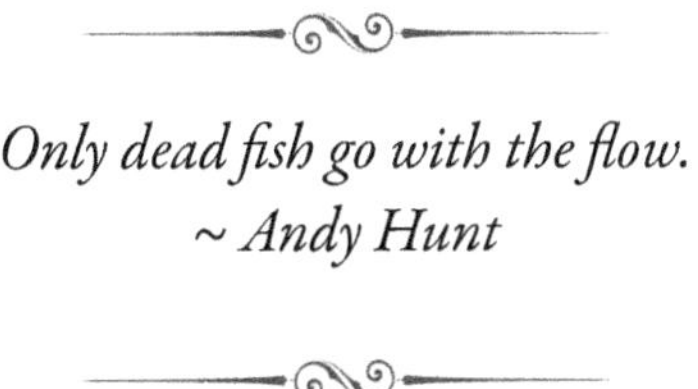

Only dead fish go with the flow.
~ Andy Hunt

Do not go where the path may lead, go instead where there is no path and leave a trail.
~Ralph Waldo Emerson

IT IS JUST LIKE BEING on a potter's wheel...there is a process of molding and shaping. Changing my beliefs change my reality for the better. I have chosen to be the change that I desired to see and leave a generational legacy and not continue the generational curse of abuse. What is your choice? What do you choose to change with your family lineage? Will it be the demon of lying, drinking, drugs, defeated attitudes, mental illness, lack of positive communication habits or another unhealthy trait? Are you sick and tired of being sick and tired of walking around in the fog and trials of life as if you have no hope?

LEARN from yesterday, LIVE for today, HOPE for tomorrow.
~Albert Einstein

I Am

I am a strength like none other. I am one reaching back helping a fellow brother or sister get on track; I am joy in the midst of pain, I am one who finds the happiness despite life's rain. I Am God's Diamond in the Rough.... I Am...The Daughter of THE GREAT I AM....

~Veronica Pryor-Faciane

Chapter 2
Broken Trust Recollections

(Ages 5 to 12)

Webster's Dictionary defines Trauma as a deeply distressing or disturbing experience. I know that there may be someone reading this book which has had an experience of someone trying to hurt or touch them in an unsolicited manner. There might be another reader who was able to get out of their situation sooner. Please never discount your experiences to other individual's situations. My experiences some may feel as, "WOW, NO WORDS!" There may be someone who has lost a family member(s) to domestic violence. It is imperative to know that We matter and our voices matter. Our stories matter, and therefore I am sharing my story. Never let your voice be silenced!

Age 5

I AM SURE YOU KNOW of a child in your family that is around the age of five. They are currently in kindergarten having the time of their lives, probably singing nursery rhymes, putting on shoes, washing their face, selecting clothes and playing with their friends. Can you visualize this beautiful child? Now, imagine that child living in fear because the man who should have loved and protected you, violated your trust. Imagine you being five again, hearing your door open at night and your father leaning over your bed. You wonder if he is checking on you, then you feel him rubbing his body part on you. Yes, he (my father) started (the incest) by rubbing his penis on my mouth. I opened my eyes, and he said, "Daddy needs you baby girl." I was confused and did not understand. I felt fear because he did not seem like the man I knew during the daytime in front of others. My birth father would preach and teach the Bible within the church, and others admired him. However, when nighttime would come, he would come into my room, take off my panties, rubbed his penis on my vaginal area and mouth areas of my body. As a little girl, I would hold my eyes closed and pray it would just end. Please God let him get tired and leave out my room. If I felt as if I was holding my breath for eternity. The tears would immediately roll down my eyes when he left. I remembered going to the bathroom and washing until I started to bleed. I felt SOOO dirty, hurt and confused. Then, I went back to my room and cried myself to sleep.

I LOCKED MY DOOR THE next night, and he was outraged. Watching the door nightly became a ritual. I did not get much sleep at all. I did not understand how easy it was to pick the lock. I was only 5 and concerned about my new little sister. My birth father told me; this was his "motherfucking" house and I better not lock his door again. He later expressed to me that if I didn't want my mom to be hurt or my baby sister, I better do as he tells me. So, night after night, after night, after night he came into my room...later he forced his penis into my mouth. I was confused as to how my mom did not know he wasn't in the room with her. I was confused as to how she did not hear me crying. I was confused as to why she started acting funny with me sometimes. What did I do? It is so sad to know that there are so many children going through this daily. If you are a teacher or adult dealing with youth, please be mindful, you never know what a child may be facing night after night.

I LOVE MY BIRTH FATHER, but he will never love me as just his daughter. Hate only destroys the person who is projecting hate towards another. You will see why I feel this way as the story progresses. It is sad how much anger my birth-father has in him. There was an article written in the online publication called Living Well, (retrieved December 2018), within this document, I learned that a man's anger could be triggered by feelings people say a "real man" should be able to control

(i.e., weakness, fear, inadequacy, sadness, powerlessness, and distress). This type of thought process placed into the mindsets of young men, can lead to self-destructive mannerisms and impact future relationships in a negative way. Especially, those who experienced sexual assault/abuse and did not report the incident, or nothing would be was done after porting it to make them feel protected or cared about.

I hear many say real men don't cry. Why? They hurt too. Upon further reading, I found that anger seems like it takes over a man's, or anybody's life. Have you ever felt like you are no longer in control of your choices? The physiological responses/effects within stressful situations can elevate tension within your body and blood pressure that can lead to aggression. Remember you should control how you express your anger or any feeling and not allow it to control you.

Age 10

THINGS PROGRESSIVELY grew worse. I remember my birth father beating on my mom, talking down to her, calling her stupid, telling her she was dumb for not being able to manage bills etcetera on a daily. If she did not cook what he wanted he would get mad as hell. Of course, he grew worse with coming into the room that I shared with my little sister. I did not want her to hear what was going on and I did not want him to touch my baby girl who was now 6, and I had two brothers who were 4 and 3. He never threatened me with hurting my baby brothers 'sexually, but he would beat them ridiculously.

AS FOR ME, HE WAS NOW kissing on my body and performing oral sex, making me sicker to my stomach. The things he did make me think of becoming more sexual to feel "normal per se." Well, I desired to have a boyfriend and for boys to notice me because I felt like something was wrong with me. I must be causing this. What is wrong with this man, this monster? How could he? I never had the experience of being treated like a princess. I will never have the experience of my father looking at me as just his daughter. Why was this happening to me? I was the daughter who helped him overcome several challenges. I helped him learn how to become a proficient reader. He had learning challenges in school even after graduation. However, that bastard's anger grew worse as each day passed, regardless of how much effort I took to help him improve his literacy skills.

Now What?

"OK, WHAT DO YOU MEAN baby girl? He did what?" I asked myself. Now, I know you may be wondering how you could not know something was happening to her (my younger sister) and she was in the same room with you. It is simple; I slept hard when I had a chance to rest. I prayed daily to not wakeup if he was in there. Now, what am I supposed to do? He is touching my sister. Damn, I don't want to tell my teachers.... I don't want to end up in the foster care system. He does not let us go anywhere. Who do I trust? Who can I tell? I did play with neighborhood children. Maybe I could tell the educators that lived next door; I did look up to their older children as my big brothers and sisters, or the judge that lived across the street. Jesus Help! He could talk so well. What if, others do not believe me?

"WELL, BABY GIRL, WE will go to mom," I said she is our only hope. He beats on her like us, but it is worth a shot." The day came, and I went to my mom with my sister. We expressed to her what was going on in detail. Finally, we will be leaving this maniac, WRONG!!! My mom said, "What do you want me to do?" Nooooooo Wordsssssss. I was confused, I was lost, and now I did not know which way to turn. I told my baby girl, "It will be ok. I will take care of you." Now, what do I do? Things did not turn out as I'd hoped.

"HOW COULD YOU MOMMA? She told him everything, like a tape recorder. He came to me more vengeful than ever! I wanted to tell my pastor, but he (my birth father) was a minister too. Could I trust him (my pastor)?" Remember, while all of this was going on, he continued (my birth father) preaching, playing his bass guitar and teaching Bible classes and Sunday school. I began to question my birth father because I knew what the Bible said about marriage and how a father should treat his wife and raise his children I asked him: "If this is ok by the Bible, "Why do I feel dirty?" Well, this is when he brought the Lord and scriptures into it. He told me I was his concubine. (He mishandled and manipulated the scriptures) Yes, that is right....and he threatened me more and more because women should not question men according to his mind. The sad thing is, there are many males (not men in my opinion) that feel this way. I felt hopeless, but I had to protect my babies'. I remember praying for my sister and brothers, so, I thought it was my fault they were born into this horrible family situation.

Hot Rice

I HAD BEEN WAITING for this day for a longggg time. He was in one of his moods and fussing at my mom. He came home daily acting like Dr. Jekyll and Mr. Hyde. She was cooking and threw a hot pot of rice at him. "Yes mama, get him!" I told myself. Guess what? She snapped and wondered how the rice got on the floor. "Are you kidding me?" I thought. What is really going on with our lives? Why is my mom not standing up for us? Why is she falling for his mind games and manipulation? Whatever you do,- stop - pause - breath - and think; who in the hell is this sort of mistreatment benefiting? Is this love when you are not being respected and experiencing constant rejection? I pray you to gain physical strength and mental clarity if you are currently experiencing this kind of abuse. If you lived through this as a child, why do you choose to live through it as an adult?

HE WOULD HAVE MY MOM believe, by vocal manipulation, that her mother did not truly love her, because she was given to her aunt, who did not have children. Momma noooo, do not believe him. Don't be so in love with others more than self, momma. This thought process is a sure-fire road to continuous unhappiness and depression. I thought, your mom was a young mother with two children, and she did love ya'll both. That man is using you, ughhhh. Can I say this to her? NOPE! I was a child, and I had to stay in a child's place. Mom, you were the only child, and they appeared to have given her everything. To me, you had it better than your siblings, because my grandfather worked for the railroad. I understand he was my Uncle biologically, but Papa Red (who raised my mother) was my Grandfather, too. I would not dare tell him. I knew he (Papa Red) would believe his daughter and I knew she (my mother) would not go against my birth father. She seemed to love this man (my birth father) more than herself.

12- My 1st Summer Job with City Parish

MY FIRST PAYING JOB was received at the age of 12 during the summer with JTPA. I determined that my siblings and I were going to be ok, but I had to do something. Since children can be bullies and we did not have uniforms in public school at that time that concerned me. People called me names just because I had long hair. Go figure; this was too much! I had to deal with no peace at home and now no peace of mind at school, too! Determined more than ever, I was going to make something out of myself and get myself and my babies out of this mess.

I WAS STATIONED TO work at our neighborhood park working with the summer campers. Going to work became the highlight of my life. Having a passion for helping others, gave me such peace. I used all my money to make sure we had school clothes. I don't remember why the adults (my parents) let me. We appeared to have financial problems I think. However, I felt after that year; they made it my responsibility to take care of our clothes. Yes, the sexual, physical and mental abuse continued. Now, we can add financial abuse to my list of hurt also as a pre-teen. Who does that to their child? Believe it or not, that is how many young males get into selling drugs. Mother's forcing their son to grow up fast and help with their siblings and household finances.

She is so tired

I REMEMBER MY MOM TRYING to call out our spelling words and check our homework. You DID NOT want his help. Why do you ask? He would beat your ass if you made a single mistake. He had no patience when he was in a rage. She worked hard to have our food cooked, house cleaned and helped us with our studies, and she did have a job outside the home also. He would fuss and hit on her, even when she was pregnant. Momma, you are a Queen.... stop allowing him to disrespect you. Don't you love yourself? Now, my momma seemed to be tired of me, too. As the years passed, I felt like we grew further apart. I just wanted to have a mother to hang out with, have our nails done and shop. Of course, now in middle school, he has started penetrating me. I am tired ya'll, Lord Please. Keeping my grades up with little or no sleep was a challenge, but I did it and then dealing with the daily dramas of just being in middle school too. The feeling of wanting to die grew more and more; however, I had to take care of my babies.

Chapter 3
When will it end?

(Ages 13 to 20)

HE WOULD SHOW ME SCRIPTURES and utilize The Bible to confuse me. He took various scriptures and distorted the meaning and convinced me via force and fear that I was his concubine. Daily, I would get up and go through the motions of pretending to be happy. I am sure many are reading this that can relate to this feeling of just going through the motions of life daily. It was a challenge keeping my grades up and putting on the appearance of being a happy family. Sad to say, as I look back over pictures from this period in my life, seeing the hurt and lack of zeal within the photographs. I could not keep a normal boyfriend like others because I could not deal with the beatings due to his jealousy. He would threaten to tell people he was fucking me. Yes, those were the words he would use. He would threaten to get me pregnant and ask me how I would explain that. He had a way of confusing me and making me feel like less than a person. Develop a plan to get away if this is your current situation. You deserve peace.

I FELT AS IF I WAS just a tool, a mere slave to only his selfish desires. I went to church, and I wondered why God was allowing this to manifest continually in my life. I was so sick of him telling my mom that he was doing this to save me. Save me my ass. I am agitated just thinking about it. If this was to protect me, why did you beat me into saying to my mom that I viewed you as my man? Yes, he did that too! My stomach is in knots. You know once your vision changes, and you look back over the things experienced, all I can say is MY GOD.

"You must never have sexual relations with a close relative, for I am the Lord. Do not violate your father by having sexual relations with your mother. She is your mother; you must not have sexual relations with her."

Leviticus 18:6-7

I saw this scripture much later in life, and of course, he never spoke about this one.

"1 You then, my son, be strong in the grace that is in Christ Jesus. 2 And the things

you have heard me say in the presence of many witnesses entrust to reliable people

who will be qualified to teach others.......... 14 Keep reminding God's people of

these things. Warn them before God against quarreling about words; it is of no

value, and only ruins those who listen. 15 Do your best to present yourself to God

as one approved, a worker who does not need to be ashamed and who correctly

handles the word of truth. 16Avoid godless chatter, because those who indulge in

it will become more and more ungodly."

~2 Timothy 2: 1-2 & 14-16

THAT IS HOW CULT-LIKE behavior can take over the minds of its followers. He teased me concerning my mixture of friends in school. I never cared about the color or race of anyone. I was confused because I saw him around acquaintances of various ethnicities too. Soooo, why did he call me a white girl? Really, birth-father! All because I desired to make something of myself. Cultivating this sort of mindset within a child is horrible. I am so glad that this seed did not take root. He insulted me on numerous occasions, saying I thought I was better than he and my mom. I believe this is one of the reasons why so many children come to school angry and totally confused within this sort of toxic environment at home.

There was an article that describes how toxic stress such as mistreatment, poverty or discrimination can adversely affect a child.

THE ARTICLE WAS ENTITLED, "*The Lifelong Effects of Early Childhood Adversity and Toxic Stress*" *published in the American Academy of Pediatrics Technical Report January 2012, Vol. 129/Issue 1, research within molecular biology, neuroscience, genomics, sociology, economics, and epidemiology was vital in understanding the materialization of various diseases across a human being's lifespan. Early toxic stress has been linked to impairments in learning, behavior, and both physical and mental well-being. It was suggested within this report that diseases can be considered as developmental disorders that materialize at the onset of one's life. With the alleviation of toxic stress within a child, there will be a reduction of health issues associated with exposure to mistreatment, poverty, and discrimination.*

Wow! Research is key to learning how to change the trajectory of my life and yours too if you choose to change. I want to live my best life and keeping those old thoughts and memories in the forefront of my mind, weighed me down during every aching second of my life at that time.

Once again, when will it end?

NOW, BACK TO WHEN WILL it end for my siblings and me? If I wanted to give certain types of gifts to my siblings, he accused me of trying to destroy them. Really??? For example, certain clothes are jewelry would make them do bad things. I was not suggesting they have their ears pierced at an early age or anything. I did not want them teased for having off-brand clothing. I was not born with a golden spoon. I had to work for our things. I remembered my next job at Popeyes working for $3.35 per hour. I worked long hours to make sure my siblings would be able to get their needs and desires covered. Working long hours took a toll on me because when I made it home, I had to perform and not be a bum fuck. Yes, if I did not do precisely what he told me, I would get beat for being a bum fuck (in his mind, that would mean not doing or moving the way he felt I should). Who was destroying who again?

The miscarriages

I REMEMBERED MY MOM had several miscarriages and after the fourth child I thought she couldn't have anymore. She would go into such a deep depression, and he would worsen with his actions, believe it or not. My mind felt as if it was going to explode. I felt that God hated me, my mom and my siblings.

I wish

I WISH I COULD HAVE lived a balanced and happy childhood. However, my life was filled with plenty of dysfunction. I wish I could have attended parties and other functions like my peers, but due to the daily drama, he did not allow us much freedom or distance from him. I was forced to live with a caged mind, heart, and soul. I would see my classmates' prom pictures and wish I could have had that opportunity. I cried for never having the chance to be a child, for never having to experience prom, if only for one night.

Promiscuity equaled normalcy...in my mind

MY DESIRE TO FIND LOVE in all the wrong places increased. There I go again trying to find normalcy. Well, at least what my mind thought was normal. In life, I have learned that my normal, was based on various circumstances and my life's daily living environment. So, ONLY GOD can judge me and you. It is not my place to point fingers, and my hope is that by reading my story, others will change their perception of others who have various life's challenges that the reader may or may not have experienced personally. Consider not to pass judgment without knowing the entire story of a person. The tables could be reversed. Have compassion even if someone is veering in the wrong direction. The light or darkness of your life/actions towards them can be a focal point in a person's decision to change.

PLEASE REMEMBER, I was going to church daily. I heard the conversations of some of the so-called church folk. The Church community's actions, within my eyes, sometimes brought up various reasons for hesitating to reaching out and seeking help. I listened to the adults talk about each other's faults. Remember, children do have ears even if they are told to be seen and not heard. I have learned to be mindful around my children. There is death and life in the power of the tongue.

THEREFORE, I WAS GRATEFUL for life being spoken into me by some of the very people I was seeking normalcy. Yes, I mean some men asked me why I was trying to use myself and not care about my body. I would get angry...just give me what I "thought" I was looking for. I PRAISE GOD for caring for me when I did not care for myself. I have never had any sexual disease or pregnancy. BUT GOD!!! I remember one summer meeting a football player at a university where I was interning who told me I deserved better than I was treating myself. God knows how to plant the seeds and the message you need to hear. It was up to me to listen. I felt convicted and horrible inside. I did not know he (a well-known football player at the university) knew of me. What kind of name was I developing? Why could I not rid myself of the negative thoughts in out of my head? Why am I continually giving up on me? That is one thing about God, during my journey, His voice grew louder within my spirit. I just did not know how to come from under the bondage that was given to me. I never wanted to have sex before being married. I never wanted to feel less than a Queen, but I felt like a whore. Is this what I was born to be?

He who finds a wife finds what is good and receives favor from the Lord.
Proverbs 18:22 (NIV)

IT IS SAD WHEN A YOUNG lady stops caring about herself. How will I ever have a good man that will love me for the true queen I desired to be and not what he made me? It is sad to use your body hoping that someone, anyone would take me out of the situation I was in. When watching the way life is projected on television etcetera, it characterizes a happy woman as one that has a man, kids and can take care of the home. This sounds like a prison to me, not life. Where is the joy in her doing things that cultivate growth in her mind, body and soul? Where is the balance in the state of life? Why can't she have everything and anything of value that she aspires to accomplish? Nothing is wrong with being a stay at home mom or dad, but if I desire more, why was I taught a man's foot should stay on my neck? Yep, that's right! I was taught this wonderful piece of information growing up too. *(in my sarcastic voice)* Now, this is how our world becomes filled with trouble people when the negative cycles are not broken within the family. I decided to formulate my own hypothesis about my life. I did lots of research trying to figure out why I could not get myself together. Why I would stay within these conditions when I felt within my heart things must get better. Yes, "FEAR" was vital in staying. I believed I would stand up to him one day and drop my balls (I know girls don't have that body part, but I was going to man-up one day). Then I would get my azz beat. I was a woman, and I had to stay in my place according to him.

THE LEGAL SYSTEM, IN my opinion, is not that child-victim friendly along with the foster care system. I have seen youth go from bad to worse situations. My mind was always thinking and trying to figure out what was best for my siblings and me even if I had to sacrifice myself for their well-being. The love of my siblings was one big thing he held over my head from my youth. Sad to say that someone who was supposed to protect me, utilized manipulation, fear, and control to keep me bound within my head.

CHILD SEXUAL ABUSE can lead to a wide variety of issues/ symptoms that include sleep issues, depression, poor self-esteem, shame, dissociative disorders, anxiety, and of course relationship challenges. These issues fall up under the classification of Posttraumatic Stress Disorder (PTSD). Yes, I have the challenge of living with PTSD. For those who wonder why someone abused sexually would become promiscuous, the American Academy of Experts in Traumatic Stress (AAETS) in an article "Sexual Abuse of Children, (n.d.)" noted the following reasons:

- ***Self-Worth is equated with promiscuity***

Within my mind, it helped me to sort of deal with the abuse and exist/survive. My trauma went on so long that I learned to be silent for my safety. Continuing to act as if all was well was required by him continually. **What went on in his house had to stay in his home.** Being sexually desirable by others allowed me to feel like I had some sort of self-worth.

- ***Promiscuity in Sexual Abuse Survivors Masks Other PTSD Symptoms***

Sex became like an addiction/escape on several levels. It allowed me to feel as if I wasn't dirty by my birth-father. When he would touch me, I would not remember the act once it began. I would become dissociative and remember going to clean myself up. I learned when reading the article that sex was like dopamine-, serotonin-, endorphin-loaded experience without the emotional attachment. I would feel loved even if it was for a short period of time, attractive, and even wanted in a strange way. I was not looking for anything long-term because I felt they would ultimately hurt me too. My birth-father hurt me so, all men would, of course, hurt me. Therefore, some ladies turn to homosexuality. This is how the devil sneaks in and adds his destruction to the foundation of society. When I started formal therapy is when I realized how I disassociated from the experiences to protect myself.

IT WAS EXACTLY LIKE a drug. The symptoms of sexual abuse were still within me in the worse form. I continuously looked for my next fix. My next sexual encounter to feel normal. I know there are some reading this who can relate to this and others who are clueless. Lord, I Thank You for Your Continued Favor and Covering. My heart is heavy, as I express my feelings. (deep breath) ......There are so many others that have been killed by their estranged sexual partners or became sick with various sexual diseases. Yet God Showered His Blessings on me and I NEVER experienced that hurt. To God be the glory and I must tell my story! Maybe someone will see that they have a chance of living their best life with peace, love, and joy unspeakable joy. At the end of each encounter, I felt emptier and more depressed. The desire to die was heightened because I never wanted to live like this. God even stopped multiple sexual partners' performance abilities to keep me. I am Grateful Beyond Measure for this.

BELIEVE IT OR NOT, he used my promiscuous actions as an excuse to continue taking advantage of me and brainwashing my mom. When he found out I was having sex with others, he told my mom, he was doing those lewd acts to save me from the streets. Damn! I thought telling him I was sleeping around would stop him. NOPE! He would beat me and tell me, "bitch you betta not bring a disease home to me!" I don't know if other people looked down on me or not and I frankly did not care. I just wanted to die! I needed help and did not know where to go. Do you currently feel this way or have you ever had this feeling before? But God!

Church Helped with Grounding Me

I KNOW THAT ONE OF my pastor's and his wife helped me become more active in the church. Their attention gives me greater peace during the mist of this ratchet storm. Later, I found out that they thought something was wrong. His wife told me they hoped I would have spoken to them. She was a teacher by trade too. It is my opinion that teachers are so imperative in helping to save the lives of many and this is why mindfulness training is so necessary within the educational curriculum, once this is my opinion.

- ***Replacing Promiscuity with Therapy for Childhood Sexual Abuse and PTSD was key***

IT TOOK ME A LONG TIME to seek assistance to recover from my childhood trauma. So, for those wondering, I still was scared to get help even once I started driving myself to school.

WHILE IN COLLEGE I remember a time when I approached my mom again about letting me get my sister and leave. I was working two jobs along with receiving financial aid; I could take care of us. Once again, she told him, and I was beaten for this. I did not understand. She would act like she did not know how to get us out of the situation and when I offered suggestions she would go tell him. Well, I understand why. He had me scared too, but I wanted to try to get out. Her spirits were broken like a well-trained slave. He worked hard to do the same to me. Upon finding out that I wanted to get my sister and leave, he made me sit on the floor and eat like an animal off the plate. Sexual acts also became more aggressive. One day...This will change.

Chapter 4
Why Lord?

As you can tell by the title of this chapter, I was still enslaved. However, I became so grateful to my Pastor's Wife during this period in my life. Let's call her Sister J. The desire to end my life subsided a little. I started working within the church, and that gave me peace. It allowed my mind to travel to a place of joy seeing and helping others.

The surest way to be happy is to seek happiness for others.
~Martin Luther King Jr.

WE STARTED TRAVELING to my family's church in the country more when my grandfather became sick. Now, I was not around her as much, and this saddened me. However, I was given a new project of working with the church choir. Ok...this is cool, but I had NEVER directed before, I only sang in choirs. However, this brought me soooo much joy and fear at the same time. I did not want to let God nor my grandfather down. Look how God was giving me His form of therapy during the midst of my storm. Don't think for one minute that the abuse ended neither.

YES, IT INCREASED EVEN more, and now that I am working as an adult, I am required to help even more financially. It is sad how my mind was so imprisoned to leave when I went to work or school. It is sad to think back on the amount of fear I had it paralyzed me from reaching out to the authorities for help. Watching certain movies and reading about the number of those who died trying to escape from those situations did not help either. I was already helping with my siblings and with food. Now, I am responsible for other bills and still be a slave for your sexual pleasures? I would ask myself. Lord Why? Why not just leave, you ask? I know you are still thinking that. Well, aren't you? For those that have not been in an abusive relationship/situation, this was my norm. I thought others were going through the same things. Then, I felt in my heart I was dirty. So, if others were experiencing this form of abuse, how were they dealing with it?

IT IS HORRIBLE THAT so many experiencing domestic violence or incest daily behind closed doors both male and female. Yes, I am speaking from a woman's point-of-view but remember my father's anger was seeded from the abuse and sexual trauma he received from an older male cousin. For those of you who are going through this, you deserve better, female or male! You are special! It does not matter what others may say about you or your story! Your peace is what matters.

I KNOW SO MANY WHO seek approval from others who have ongoing issues. We, yes me included, worked to buy others love. We put our emotions and feelings aside, with the hopes of the abuser to show us the respect and love we desire. By this, I mean that everyone has their perception or definition of what love means to them. Mentally, this can be a challenge because we are all individuals having various individualized thoughts on what is or feels like true happiness and love. In my opinion, this can cause problems in building relationships throughout life without proper communication and accepting other people's differences. **People often listen for hearing and not understanding** of what a specific person is trying to communicate.

"Most people do not listen with the intent to understand; they listen with intent to reply."
~Stephen R. Covey

THE SKILL OF LISTENING should be taught along with mindfulness for the development of more successful functioning generations. Just think about many times people enter disagreements due to miscommunication and incorrect assumptions about what they assume someone might be saying. It is best always to seek clarification.

Listening as defined by Merriam-Webster's online dictionary consist of a physical as well as mental process, learned and active process. When listening, a person is focused, voluntary and intentional during this process.

Hearing is defined by Merriam-Webster's online dictionary consist of a physical process that is natural and passive. When hearing a person is accidental, involuntary and does not put effort into this process.

WITHIN ARISTOTLE'S work Nicomachean Ethics, he spoke on the concept of love. The basis of his work was on achieving happiness in relation to virtue. Aristotle's thought that virtue was key to the pursuit of happiness. His belief was grounded on the fact that self-love is a precursor to loving others which is in alignment God's law and my belief's

30 LOVE THE LORD YOUR God with all your heart and with all your soul and with all your mind and with all your strength. 31 The second is this: 'Love your neighbor as yourself.' There is no commandment greater than these."
~ (Mark 12:30-31 ~NIV)

SELF-LOVE, IN MY OPINION, is key to love or lack of love within society today. My birth father had no love of self, and this was passed on to me by his

actions. I had to become mindful that I could not control him; however, I can control my thoughts and actions daily.

REMEMBER, HURT PEOPLE tend to want to hurt people, and people who are healed can assist with the healing process of others. Therefore, I continue to be transparent. He was abused and treated in a horrible manner growing up. I remember him continually saying, "Why my mom let this happen to me." His birth father was not in his life due to his mother's actions. Do you see how issues can pass from one generation to the next? He was an adult dealing with issues from his youth that is affecting his present. So reader, can you relate to something that happened when you were going up, that still is causing you issues? Are you still not living entirely in the present due to memories and thoughts of incidents that hurt you as a child?

I HAVE HEARD PEOPLE ask others close to me, why would she talk about this? Why should I allow the poison of the past to linger within me? My question to them is why does it matter if I do or do not talk about this subject matter? Is it something that you are hiding? Have you experienced a trauma that you were told to move on from by someone who should have protected you? Where you taught that what goes on within our family says within our family? Transparency and speaking my Truth is Key to My Healing and you as well. If you have an infection, aren't antibodies prescribed to help with the healing process? Speaking my truth releases the poison embedded within me by my birth father. I matter! When will you start to question yourself and matter? Dear reader, remember you matter. Mama Gayle taught me those that matter, don't mind and those that mind, don't matter. Please remember that. That was a very insightful lesson learned. Thank you again, Mama Gayle. Now, others' opinions of me, would not continue to poison my belief system.

The Choir Director

WELL BACK TO THE STORY, I started directing at one church, and after a period of years and God's elevation, I was blessed to direct a choir for another church. Lord this was the high I needed to keep myself. Yes, that is right! I stop having numerous sexual encounters. God Stepped in and said enough is enough little girl! I still felt dirty each time my birth father used my body. He would accuse me of always having multiple partners, and this gave him a reason to "help me" or should I say continue to help himself to me in his twisted mind. The sad part is, that was his story, and he stuck to it. He insisted the reason he kept raping me, was to save me from self-destruction. REALLY??

He had my mom so scared and mad. I could tell she was angry and hurt, at times she would not talk to me. I did not understand why. I was being abused just like she was. On numerous occasions, my mom would slam cabinets when he came into my room. I remember one time he told her "bitch if you don't stop I will beat you, this is my pussy, and I will take it anytime I want it!" Yes, I know, what a sick bastard.

HE WOULD BEAT ME EVERY time his mind told him I slept around. However, in hindsight, I would not touch someone who could possibly give me a disease. He did not care. He kept telling me I was his property; his concubine and his abuse/torture kept me in fear. Oh, just to let you know, he would rape me often right before going to church to preach and I better not show signs that something was wrong or else. He would go to play music in the church and teach and preach like nothing was wrong. He fooled so many within the church body and seen in society today. They deceived so much that well that will be told later within the story. Let's say he was very charismatic when he taught the Bible. It was sad he did not live everything he preached.

IT IS SHAMEFUL THAT there are so many people professing and not possessing Christ-Like Qualities and in my, this is what causes many who need help to not go to the church building for assistance. It is of my opinion that those who are in leadership should understand that it is ok to seek mental assistance. Do not make individuals feel like their walk with God is wrong because they need therapy. There are those leaders making parishioners question their faith because of their personal opinions. I loved working with my children so much within the church because there are adults that don't have the patience to listen to them.

ADULTS ARE NOT GENUINELY open with children and choose to have the "do as I say do" attitude and not as I do. Therefore, we are losing future generations because of this belief. If you don't take the time to listen to the children, how can you help them grow into confident and productive adults? Be honest with your children. Transparency expressing the good, bad and ugly about your path to adulthood helps guide others facing something similar and hopefully change the direction of future generations. All my choir babies are my children, and I loved them as my own. This love gave me the strength to make it through my abuse.

My directing was therapy, and I did not even know it at the time. It kept my mind from just focusing on the abuse. I guess this feeling gave a more precise understanding to the saying an idle mind is the devil's workshop. When I was preparing songs and learning music to teach, it gave me a sense of purpose. The negative thoughts were not as prevalent as they were before. I was feeling peace during the storm. I loved directing all ages, but I loved my babies the most. I would pour my heart into seeing them succeed and enjoy singing in the choir.

Chapter 5

Has my way out finally come?

I STARTED BECOMING extremely ill due to the stress of working long hours at the gas company. Not getting sleep at home because of the late-night abuse took a toll on my body. The doctor told me my blood pressure was going to be the death of me if I did not get the stress of my job off my plate. He did not know about the abuse going on. I used this to tell my birth father I had to find another job. I thought about it and I decided to ask my brother if I could move with him. He did not know what was going on. I never wanted my brothers to lose their lives trying to save me once they were older. I thought my way through and it seemed logical to find a job away from this monster, so I could live. I thought finally, I can get out of this situation.

I went from a very high paying job to working with the state as an auditor. I remember the person interviewing me asking if I was sure and did I understand about the tremendous pay reduction I was going to receive. Money wasn't everything, I just needed out. I could not take it anymore. I NEEDED PEACE!!

I AM FINALLY OUT OF that situation. I understand Joyce Meyer's book the Battlefield of the Mind. I was physically out of the situation but trying to truly live was hard. My mind was still in prison. The bondage of the mind was more devastating than living with him. I moved in with one of my sibling's and I was feeling better. I never told my brothers what I was going through. They were getting bigger and I did not want them to go to jail because of him. They were worth so much more to me than that. That will be another book all to itself, because they were extremely mad and hurt when they did find out. I only wanted to protect my siblings from any form of danger and my birth father used that against me.

THE CALL

THIS PERIOD OF FREEDOM was short lived once I received a devastating phone call. Wait What? What do you mean my mom may not live? I was told to come to the hospital that was over 1 hour away from where I currently lived. Once I arrived, the brain doctor on duty told me if she lives, my mom will be a vegetable. Lord, what? Can you imagine getting this news? My head was spinning. He told me he knew my father had done something but had no physical proof. I looked at him like a deer in headlights. He later explained that both main arteries at the base of her brain were severed due to a blunt trauma. My mom's body was shutting down from both ends on the ride to the hospital.

DEEP BREATH, EVERYTHING was placed into my lap again. My birth father act as if he was so hurt and distraught. I was so angry at him. I knew he had beaten her. My mom did not fall in the tub. Ohhhh why won't you just die man was my feeling at that time. I was numb and confused. I was scared to go and get clothes for her with him. I wanted to just die. The way he looked at me made my skin crawl. This man's hurt was destroying everyone close to him. There are so many family lineages experiencing destruction due to the decisions of their ancestors.

I CALLED MY BIOLOGICAL paternal-grandfather for help. He had just recently been released from the hospital. I can always say, no matter when I called, he would be there once we started spending more time together. Remember, we did not see our family members often. Isolation was key for him to keep us in fear. I wished so he was around when we were growing up. I was too scared to even tell him what I, what we have been going through.

ONE THING I CAN SAY was that my mom was a miracle! She whispered the next day after surgery, what happened? The doctors were amazed. BUT GOD!

However, I feared for her continued safety upon release. I began to feel like God really hated me too. Why am I being placed in the realm of harm again? The anxiety and panic attacks grew worse. I had not been at my new job long and I loved the people there. My desire to just feel loved allowed me to become attached to individuals very easily.

Really Man?

WOULD YOU BELIEVE, that after I moved, he never tried to get a job to keep up the bills at the house? REALLY, THIS IS TOO MUCH MAN! He believed women were responsible for taking care of him while he studies the Bible. No, for, he told me this. After, working so hard to find a grant to get our home repaired you really did nothing to keep it. Well, I did my best to save it, but I could not financially, and he did not try to lift a finger to help. They eventually ended up moving and I was obligated to take care of them once again I had little brother still in secondary school. Who was going to take care of him? I had to start taking antidepressants. My mom was very frail, and I could not stand the sight of him.

The Back-Road Nightmare

ONE EVENING, MY MOM asked me to drive her to the store, she could not drive after that horrible trauma. I told her ok momma. Guess what happened? He told me to wait he was going too! Why Lord? I will be safe, won't I? I mean, my mom is still sick. He can't be that cold hearted, can he? What could possibly happen? I am going to be ok. Would he try to hurt me again? Well, as I was driving down a long 2 lane road in a country area, he told me to pull over the van. He then made my mom. Yes, that sick.......no words man.... made my mom drive the van while he raped me!

SORRY, BUT I DON'T remember if we made it to the store or not. Remember, those going through trauma experience disassociation. I felt like I blanked out and ended up in the tub cleaning myself until I was raw. This man loved to control women. I don't know what his mom allowed to happen to him, but he projected his anger constantly towards females. He had no respect for them. Not even his own daughters. His own flesh and blood. Have you experienced something like this or know someone that has? Hurt people continue to hurt people and their anger is often misdirected.

Enough Dammit!

WELL FEBRUARY 16, 2002, I had enough of this pain. However, the way I decided to end my hurt was not the best decision. Can you guess what I tried? Leaving, nope. Telling someone in authority, nope. Well I think you know by now I tried to take my life. This was a joyous day for one of my cousin's, her wedding day. Everything my birth father could do to run anyone or friend he felt I confided in had to go in his mind. I was sick of this man and I was not going to take his life and go to jail. I had tried not to take the medication that I had to help with the depression and anxiety I had been experiencing along my life's journey. Well, after the wedding he was ranting and shouting as usual. Once he went to clean up, I placed my plans into action. I took several bottles of pills and drank a bottle of liquid codeine.

HE CAME INTO MY ROOM and began fussing and calling me out of my name again. I smiled and told him no more. You will not hurt me anymore. All I can say is God used him to watch me. I was told I was talking out of my mind and they had to charcoal me (this process stops the drugs I swallowed from being absorbed within my system, by use of a feeding tube). I should have died based on my conversation with the coroner. He told me whatever God has for me to do, I better get it done. Once again, God knows how to send his messengers to you. I was so mad at God. When my birth parents came to get me after inpatient therapy, he started all over again with making fun of me and how I handle life.

For those of you wondering, no he did not stop the molestation. I was so pissed at God. I remember cursing God. I thank God for still showing me favor. Several months later, I meet my future husband. He tried to run him off and cause all types of issues, but what God had for me it was for me. My birth father tried to destroy my wedding day. He raped me the morning of. His attitude was horrible. NOTHING HE COULD SAY OR DO WOULD MESS UP MY DAY. It was raining on this day and that was God showering his blessings on us. I loved my husband so much. But, I had to tell him something. I had to tell him my horrible lifelong secret. I should have said something before our wedding and I did not, but I did the night we were driving to the hotel. I told him everything. I was purging my system and you know what he said. He said, "He loves me and was not going anywhere." He also told me he started having ideas something was wrong, but I did not say anything. Look at God! I Thank God for my King David daily! Wait until you hear from him the things he faced as the husband of someone who suffered this form of abuse. Yes, David will be writing a book also.

What could he be thinking?

ANOTHER THING, MY BIRTH father had not given up even after I was married. One weekend, my mom kept calling my phone; however, when I answered she hung up. I told David something is wrong. I tried to call her back multiple times. I just figured I would try to talk to her when I went to rehearsal. Well, I would not have to wait for rehearsal to figure out why she was calling. Can you guess who popped up unannounced? You got it my birth father! I don't remember telling you, but he started at a young age asking me if daddy ever need you will you be there for him.

ONE OF OUR VEHICLES was in the shop and my husband normally works on the weekend. Well, this weekend, he was off. I went to lay down and I told David my concerns. Not a good 10 minutes later, we heard a knock on the door and the sides of the house. I thought it was the police knocking or something. I bet you can't guess who that was. Wow, you are good! It was my birth father. David went to answer the door and boy was he surprised. He said, "David you're home!" David told him of course Doc, where else am I supposed to be? David told him to hold on let him put some clothes on. When he went back he was gone.

DAVID CAME BACK INSIDE and told me that was my birth father. What! I told David that my mom was trying to warn me. My aunt's asked David about him coming over. David said he told them I was being kept from him. He was sick in the mind. I became extra cautious now. My aunt became extra concerned also. I ran the streets with her older sister my, but I stopped doing lots of things for my safety.

HE TRIED TO USE MY mom to bring us closer to him in my opinion. She wanted to talk to us (me and my sister) for him in my opinion. The first question she asked was do we want him to be our father? Ok...let's think about this and his past actions. I told my mom, I love him from a distance and we don't have a daddy daughter relationship because of his actions. Not mine. I was so mad the she seemed to be caught in the middle. He always uses my mom. He preys on weaker people and he is paying for that. Remember, you always reap what you sow.

Chapter 6
Domestic Violence Facts/ Signs

There are so many people living in denial. They feel that they can change the hearts of their abuser. To what extent are you willing to sacrifice your life and/or your children's life and future to stay in a toxic relationship?

Do you know some signs of abuse?

ACCORDING TO AN ARTICLE written in Psych Central (retrieved on December 27, 2018) women, men and children are affected physically, psychologically and socially. The abuser utilizes intimidation, fear along with verbal and physical acts of violence. My birth father was very good at this. He would keep us isolated from family and friends. He kept on top of all our associates. The mind control was the worst thing ever. My mom could not get the thoughts of not leaving nor protecting and standing up to him out of her head. She chose to stop eating to stop those thoughts. She transitioned March 23, 2015.

THE VICTIMS OF DOMESTIC violence no longer have control over their own lives within their own home. Pretending daily that all is well, because the abuse threatens you if anyone should find out what is going on behind closed doors.

Within the same article in Psych Central (retrieved on December 27, 2018) it was noted that child abuse and domestic violence tends to happen within the same family. Researchers have noted that 50% to 70% of the men who frequently assaulted their wives also frequently abused their children. Which according to the statistics, when a partner is being abused the children are 1,500 time likely to be abused also.

THESE CHILDREN OFTEN experience 6 times higher suicide rates, a 24% higher chance of committing sexual assault crimes, 50% higher chance of abusing alcohol and drugs, and those that witness the abuse of their mothers tend to take on violent behavior themselves. Like I learned in accounting, garbage in garbage out. Adults please be mindful when you are in contact with youth. You never know what they are going through, and they are our future. Just making the opportunity to listen to them even if you are going through something may change the trajectory of their life. Remember, it did for me. I remember a child telling me how grateful he was I listened to him, because after his new sibling arrived, he felt like his parents did not have time for him. Where would this world be if we regained the village mentality once again?

Signs of Abuse

OK, LET'S TOUCH ON the signs of abuse that some may or may not pay attention to. I will talk about the signs documented within the Psych Central article (retrieved on December 27, 2018) and so, things I did to help try to cover up the abuse. There are those that experience numerous outward injuries with broken bones, bruises etc. Those individuals try to pass it off as I fell, or they are being clumsy and ran into something.

I AND SO MANY OTHERS kept headaches, pelvic pain, numerous frequent vaginal and urinary tract infections, gastrointestinal (stomach and intestine) problems and various eating disorders. I also met people who tried to numb their pain with inflicting cuts to various areas of their skin. I developed lots of unanswered aches and pains, anxiety, stress and horrible depression. Along with this your body can develop various other diseases because you are not in balance and living a life of unrest.

A Victim assessment?

PLEASE CONSIDER ANSWERING the following to see if you or someone you may know maybe a victim of domestic violence. If you answer yes, please consider seeking help. I will list some possible places to seek assistance.

1. Are you in a relationship in which you have been physically hurt or threatened by your partner?

1. Has your partner ever hurt your pets or destroyed your clothing, objects in your home or something special to you?

3. Has your partner ever threatened or abused your children?

1. Have you been forced you to have sex when you did not want to?
2. Are you forced to engage in sexual acts that make you feel uncomfortable?
3. Are you afraid of your partner?
4. Does your partner ever prevented you from leaving the house, seeing friends, getting a job or continuing your education?
5. Has your partner ever used or threatened to use a weapon against you?
6. Does your partner constantly criticize you and call you names?

IF YOU HAVE ANSWERED yes to any of the above, seek help. You are worth your peace, joy- and protection. You matter! Please call the National Domestic Violence Hotline 1-800-799-7233 or 1-800-787-3224 (TTY) if you are unaware of any one to seek assistance from in your local area. If you are international, then you make can speak to amnesty international within your area for guidance. The important thing to do is get help. Call local authorities or go to your local hospitals for help. Do not stay in a violent situation. Even if you don't believe you desire better YET, trust me, you do! You really do. So, for others that have not experienced this, please be mindful of your opinions. When someone stays within this sort of situation, there is something missing within them internally. Self-Love is missing.

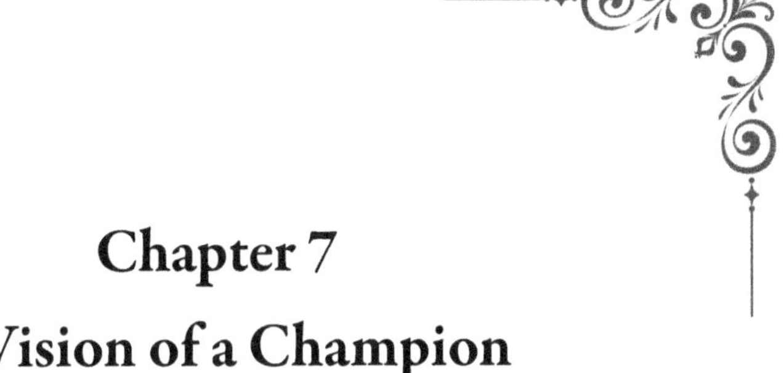

Chapter 7
A Vision of a Champion

I Will Break **the abuse patterns, will you?**

Some may not know how the cycle of abuse works. So below is a diagram that explains the process. To rectify a problem or issue, you must admit there is an issue.

THIS CYCLE WHEN CONTINUED, destroys the future and lives of family's, thus carrying on generational curses/challenges. Ending this process is not an easy task. I am not going to lie to you and say pray and it alllll will end. Faith without works is dead. Thus, I can have all the faith I want, until I acted I stayed within that vicious cycle.

AFTER ADMISSION OF abuse, I had to develop a plan or vision to change. I wanted God, as I am sure many others do as well, to miraculously lift me out of this situation. God says whosoever will.....My self-will was so weak, my spirit was so broken. BUT GOD!! I cannot continue living and feeling like this. I had no balance within my life. I had to develop my Vision of a Champion. If you desire change, you must develop your vision as well. Are you tired of just settling for the known hell you are choosing to live in daily? Why continue to be afraid of change and moving to the unknown heaven? So many speak about faith and that is exactly what change consist of along with action. People tend to **settle** for the **known hell** then chance changing for the **Unknown Heaven**. Where is your faith? Well.....answer self. How can you move towards your truth if you are not 100 percent true to yourself? You can lie to lots of people, but when you lie to self, which is the ultimate self-sabotage, you are abusing/hurting yourself in my opinion. Don't you think it is time to take off your mask? What is your true refection when you look into the mirror?

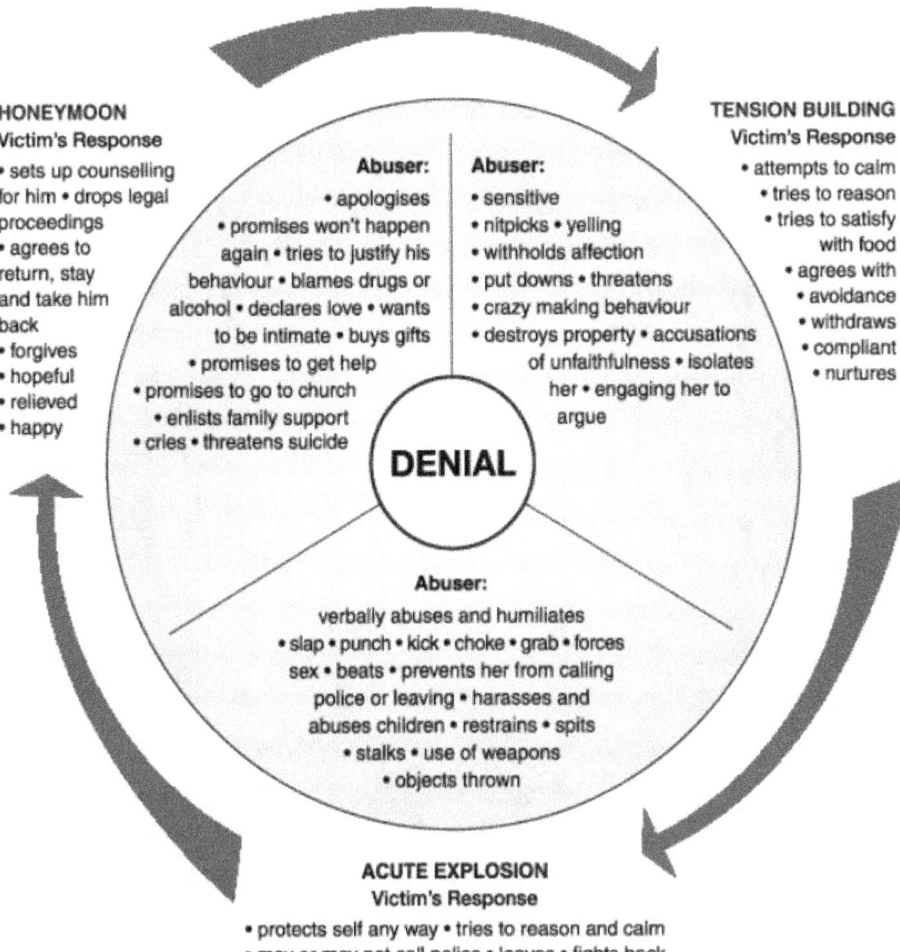

Cycle of Violence

The Challenges of Wanting Change

I HAD BEEN MARRIED for a short period of time and found out I was pregnant. Look at God! Due to damage within my body, I was told I would not be able to have children. I still faced challenges with my birth father. Every girl wants her mom to be there when she is finding out the sex of her child. Well, my mom told me she was coming, and I sat outside the hospital waiting for her. She never showed up and I almost missed my appointment. He told me, I told you your mom will never disobey or go against me. In my opinion he was very narcissistic. He wanted to control everything and to think that I still had hope he would change. God fixed it for my mom to be there during my first son's birth, without him. I will always cherish that moment. God was continually giving me the desires of my heart and I still was not happy.

I just want to be happy

Take delight in the Lord, and He will give you the desires of your heart.
~Psalms 37:4 (NIV)

I JUST WANTED TO BE happy! During this phase of my life, I had two sons and a very loving husband; however, my mind was still not at peace. I was tired of the fighting going on with the thoughts in my head. I continually worried about what happened to me and if I was going to be safe. I was a grown woman in statue, but I was a distraught little girl in spirit.

BY NOW, MY HUSBAND and brother-n-law, at that time, had confronted my birth father about what they knew. He was made aware that he was not welcomed to our homes unless invited. He was totally stunned. He thought they called him over because they were having issues with us. He told me my marriage would never work and that I was going to do something to fuck it up like I do everything else in my life. He was the one tearing me apart. He was the one that tried to destroy is family due to his inward anger. They had to confront him. On numerous occasions, we noticed him in the vicinity our home, but he would keep going. I did not know if I should get a restraining order or not. God why is this happening to meee? I felt the ink written on a restraining order had no value in my safety.

ONE DAY, ONE OF MY aunts told me I needed to check on my mom. She thought he had done something to her. Well, she was right, and I could not figure out what. I called my brother and told him my concern about mom and he road with me to check on her. My mother just kept saying that she was not me and appeared to be talking out of her head. My birth father wanted to manipulate his children against each other. Yes, I know. I have no words also. Well my mom had to go to get help and he became very angry with me. He told me I could not keep his wife from him. I was so sad when she was released, and she said she had to go back to him. I could see the fear in her eyes when she told me I don't understand. Mom......No don't go back. I can't help you there. I was so lost and confused. I know the fear she felt by not returning. I have been there. My blood pressure medication was not working, and I felt like a total failure. Why can't I save my momma?

He threatened my husband

HE ACCUSED MY HUSBAND of doing something to me because of everything David confronted him with. My birth father told him that girl would never say any of those things without being forced to. When David told me this I was speechless. Now, this man, my birth father really believed he knew me better than I knew myself. I am sure if you are going through something currently or in the past, your abuser felt or feels the same way. What makes this ironic is he told David he was going to teach him how to keep his foot down on my neck. David told him he was crazy, and he respects women. My birth father told David he will learn. You don't know how to handle women the right way. David told him Doc, I don't want to learn anything you have to teach. The respect I had for you, as a man and self-professed minister of God, is no longer there. David in my opinion, is a true example of a strong Christian man.

Saving Mom

I HAD MADE MY MIND up to do something to save her. I just did not know what I was going to do at that specific point in time. Later, I decided to press charges. I had to get my mindset together for this. I knew that people were going to pass their opinions and judgment. My mind had to be set and ready for anything and everything. I had no idea some of the things I would face BUT GOD! I thought people would say this was something I wanted because of my age at the end. I thought people would believe him over me because of his very charismatic attributes. I thought and thought and thought until finally, I did not give a damn what people would say.

I DID NOT TELL MY HUSBAND the day I went to file a statement with the police. My heart was being prepared for the worse. I was surprised that he was already being investigated for touching my little cousin that had been in his care. WOW look at God! After, I found out that, I did not want her to go through anything else. So, I tried to take the brunt of everything. Fear is a fool, but I had to press on.

The night he was arrested

NO WORDS ABOUT HOW I was feeling. Shock, dismay, relief, scared and so many other emotions were going through me. I remember crying in David's arms and being up all night. I had to try to keep it together with work and life. That was quite a challenge during this period. The day after his arrest the drama began. No family wants their name to be tainted, but the generational curse had to end. I was called a liar and could go to jail by some. Later, they came and apologized, but all was well in my heart already. They did not live one piece of my story. I did not give a damn what they thought, frankly. I just wanted to save my mom. I knew it was going to be a long road. My birth father could be very convincing and so many people loved and looked up to him. I had some ask me why I did not come to confine in them. All I can say is may the life you live speak for you. No one is perfect, but if your character is questionable, why would I trust you? Trust is earned and so does mutual respect.

HELLO VERONICA, YES, he admitted what he did. Wait, he did what? When I spoke with the police contact and they said he admitted to so much I was amazed. If you are deciding to stand up for yourself, remember to stand even if you must stand alone. You are worth it!

DURING THIS PROCESS, my mom came to stay with me. I watch him try to manipulate her concerning me dropping the charges. The calls she received started tearing her apart more and more. I watched how he manipulated his way to find other ways to call her and talk down to her. She would go to visit him, and she would come home so sad and depressed. The last time she ever visited him, he was beating on the jail bars yelling at her. Remember, he always called her a stupid bitch and would tell her she would never be anything. The sad part is I remember my mom telling him, I would stay with you even if we did not have a penny between us. It was so sad to see her love him more than she loved herself. This is why so many women stay in the confines of a domestic violence situation so long. Men if you have been hurt, don't take your anger out on someone you feel is weak. One day you may just be surprised. God judges the hearts of men/women pass your test. Stop the perpetuation of abuse and hurt. It is ok for you to cry. You matter!

MY MOM'S HEALTH STARTED to go down very rapidly with depression. She was perfectly healthy, but as reality set in that he was going to jail for a long time she went into a shell. They sentenced him to 30 years at my request. They wanted to give him much more time for all the counts he had. On the initial paperwork there was 50 counts of incest, 50 counts of forcible rape and 3 counts of sexual battery. I want you to know that only accounted for the period after they moved when my mom became sick in 2000. I never went to press charges in the parish of my youth. I felt that was punishment enough for the hurt he caused and his current age at sentencing.

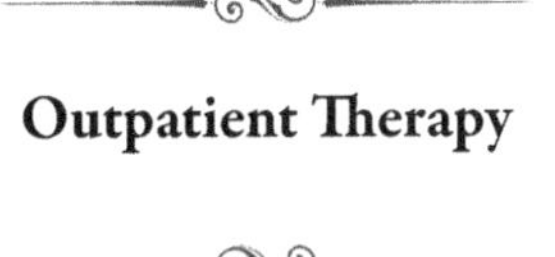

Outpatient Therapy

Lord I am tired. I could not focus a work, home and life in general. I was tired from everything that has happened within the course of my life thus far. I did not like having sexual relations with my husband, because it constantly reminded me of what happened to me. What the Hell!! David is nothing like that animal. If I don't pull it together, he is going to leave. I remembered someone telling me, what you won't do another woman will. Jesus Help! I would come home on Friday's and sleep all weekend. I was suffering from very severe depression. *I stayed in my mind trying to figure out what was wrong with me.* Don't ever do that if you want peace and growth within you. Work on always living in the present. Not the past nor the future (that would bring on major anxiety). My husband would come home from work and take care of the children. I had no drive to do anything. I did not want to live, but I loved my children and husband. I knew they deserved better. I Thank God for my boss and coworkers at during this time. They were my support system. I will Never Forget what they did for me. I was put to the refiner's fire to catapult me to my NEXT. My family became my "WHY" for change.

IN AN ARTICLE WRITTEN by Lauren Hardy, MA. (2014), she spoke about various treatment available for those facing the challenge of depression. There are individuals that need a combination of treatment options with their level of care. I know that I did. When you have depression, antidepressants help to increase the levels of neurotransmitters within individuals. I had to have a combination of medication to help with depression, anxiety, stress, focus and sleeping. I also went to outpatient therapy. This was a challenge, because having an active support system is what most people feel they need just to get moving. Well, my husband did not believe that talking to someone was going to help me. He felt I should just move on, but I did not know how to. Not talking about my feelings did not mean I did not have any feelings or thoughts. Those thought were crippling my life.

Control your thoughts on a daily basis and don't allow your thoughts to control you in order for you to live your best life.
~Veronica Pryor-Faciane

Did You Know?
You can "Rewire" your brain to be happy by simply recalling 3 things you're grateful for every day for 21 days.
~Holistic Ali

DO YOU CURRENTLY FEEL like this? Like there is no hope, living with constant unexplained aches and pains. Well, that was me. I had several surgeries and I believe now that it was stress and anxiety induced issues. The reason is because I still had some of the same issues after the surgeries. Your mind unsettled can wreak havoc within your body. It did mine.

In an article entitled, "The Effect of Depression in Your Body," it was noted that depression is a common mental health issue affecting 26 percent of the adults in the United States. Even though depression is a mental health issue, the effects of this illness can manifest in your physical health like it did me. Whatever you do, get help. I know my birth father made fun of me when he found out I was utilizing medication to help me. He should have been doing the same thing in my opinion. Depression if not treated can affect:

- Insomnia

- Feelings of emptiness and sadness

- focused on death or hurting oneself

- Cognitive issues with focus and memory

- Feel clingy

- Stress causes constricted blood vessels which increases risk of heart attack

- Stomach issues

- Weight fluctuations (under/over eating)

- Fatigue

- Lower sex drive

- Weak immune system

THE POSSIBILITIES OF disease are heightened when your body is not at ease or is imbalanced. Please don't forget to always talk with your children. To change the cycle or trajectory of a family, we cannot forget about the children. I know I use to hear that children should be seen and not heard, but you don't know what is going on if you don't allow them to speak. I know it is a challenge dealing with your own trials and tribulations, but we must slow down and stay in the present (be mindful) for our future generations.

OUTPATIENT THERAPY was hard work, but it was worth it! I know people all have their opinions about therapy, but The Bible says with the mind I serve the Lord. How can you serve the Lord if your mind is sick? Don't you go to the dentist if you have a toothache? Don't you go to see your podiatrist if your feet or foot hurts? Don't you go to your primary care if you are having issues with diabetes, high blood pressure or need a shot for a sinus infection? Don't you....well you get the picture. So, if your mind is having issues and it controls the ENTIRE BODY why do you not go to the therapist? I'm just saying. Well?

I Can't Do This Roni

IT REALLY HURT ME TO see my mom give up on life. She started feeling bad because she had been scared to get out of that abusive relationship. Prior to my mom's transition, she stopped eating and said she could not do this anymore. She was tired of all the thoughts and memories she could not erase from her head. I would be called to check on her while at work because of the things she was saying. The social worker was concerned. When I heard what she was saying, I explained she was talking about incidents that transpired over the course of her life with my birth father. My mom shut her body down by allowing her thoughts to control her and imprison her mind.

IT HURT SO BAD WHEN she looked at my sibling's and me and said please let me go. Go where momma? In my mind I had an idea, but I wanted clarity. I she said Veronica you know exactly what I am talking about. I cried myself to sleep that night. I felt like I had totally failed my momma. How am I supposed to stay strong for my babies'/siblings? I watched my mom transition slowly from here. The hardest thing was preparing for your mother's funeral when she could have changed her transition date with a change in mindset. Ordering a coffin, her dress etcetera. During this period, I worked on strengthening my mind for her day. I talked to my doctor about anxiety medication to handle it when the time came, just in case.

AFTER WE HAD TO TAKE the feeding tube out, it was a matter of time. She stopped talking and responding all together. I would go back and forth to the living assistance facility to spend time with her. I knew she could hear me. She felt alone her entire life, I was determined not to let her transition alone. The children had gone to visit her Sunday, March 22, 2015, after church. No, she was not responding. My heart was so sad. Her bodily functions were no longer working. She had no fluids in her system and she was on oxygen to help her shallow breathing. Mama, please change your mind. I pleaded with her. I never had the chance to have a normal mother and daughter relationship. Please mama get up.... Monday, March 23, 2015, I called David at work. I explained I was feeling something, and I was not going to let her be alone. I WAS NOT! I went directly to my mom after work. I laid next to her praying for a miracle. Not seeing that when you are not at peace in your mind, you are imprisoned. The doctors told me she could not last much longer like this. That was the hardest thing ever to do, but I had to be strong. (Tears) I told her I had to go home fix dinner and help the children with homework. I said, "Mama, I will be back...don't you go home without me. I don't want you crossing over alone. I love you Mama...I will be right back."

I RUSHED HOME AND TOOK care of everything I needed to then David stayed with the children. I called my siblings to tell them I think Mama is crossing over. I had to watch the terms I used for my mental strength. Using the "d" word (dead) was not going to work for me. I believe our spirit lives on and this shell of a home (body), goes back to the dirt. I know this would not be our final time seeing each other. None of my siblings wanted to hear that message from me. I told them I was going to be by her side and I will call ya'll to keep you posted.

As her time drew near, her breath was slower and shallow. I sat up and started talking to her as fast as I could. I let her know how much I loved her and to please just be happy and love on her mothers, fathers, and our other siblings she miscarried. Her last breath...wait Mama.... Mama...I laid on her to see if I could feel her heart. My heart skipped a beat. I went to get the nurse. She confirmed what I thought...Lord, I must call my babies' and tell them Mama has transitioned to her next phase of life.

THIS IS JUST A SIDE note concerning "death" (chills). That word seems so final to me. For me to be at peace and not linger in mourning I choose to utilize the word transitioned. It is a healthier word for my mental state of wellbeing.

NOW, THE STAFF TURNED the air low and I called my siblings and the funeral home. My sister told me to get up. No.... I am never going to feel her warm again...Just a little while longer. They packed her things and my brother told me to come on. No, I am not going to leave her until the funeral home comes to get her. Till we meet again Mama. Her death will not be in vain.

IF JUST ONE PERSON decided to get mental help, then writing this book was worth it. Telling my story is an important part of my healing process too. The next and final chapter of this book will discuss the steps I utilized for my healing journey of which I am still traveling. **Remember to be mindful and take notes.** This is my process, but you are the one who will draft your roadmap. You are the one who will have to do the work to become your best-self. No matter how many therapist or doctors you go to, if you don't follow the prescription, the healing process will never begin. Ok.... let's head to the last chapter to see what prescriptions I used. Always remember you are not alone! If you have went to formal therapy and seek assistance with the development of your roadmap, my contact information will be located at the end of the book.

Chapter 8
The Roadmap to my New Beginning

My Vision is Clearer

THANK GOD, I HAVE MADE it this far amidst life's continuous obstacle course. Pushing past my usual procrastination wall, has been a very fulfilling accomplishment. (deep slow breath to bask in gratitude) I would stall on progressing for the fear of possible failure. I became so accustom to hearing the negative programming from my birth father, until I started believing it. There goes a thought that I had to get under control to move to my greater. Now, having a different prospective/thought of failure has played an insurmountable roll in my transformation. The following quotes just about sums up how I feel currently about the thought of failure:

Failure is Only the Opportunity to Begin Again, Only This Time, More Wisely.
~Henry Ford

Success is The Ability to go from one failure to another with No Loss of Enthusi-
asm.
~Winston Churchill

Failure is Not the Opposite of Success, It's Part of Success.
~Author Unknown

THIS JOURNEY HAS NOT been easy, but ohhhh it was soooo worth it! (deep breath) Deep slow breathing allows me to slowdown my thoughts and **not allow** them (my thoughts) to run around in my head like a bunch of bad ass kids (lol).

WE ALL HAVE EXPERIENCED various trials and tribulations, joy and laughter, and often great pain and loss. Trust me, the number of horrible deaths my family has experienced on both sides have been – (deep breath), very trying. For me to not allow a continuous grieving spirit to control my thought, I had noticed the thought and re-craft my thought that death was is not the end. However, the thought was crafted to see my love one as only transitioning to their next phase of life. This helped me so much with dealing with my mom's transition. It is up to us as individuals to walk gracefully through life's challenges or be buried within life's events as if we have no hope. To God Be the Glory for all He has, is, and will do within my life and yours too! It is all up to you. So, are you thinking about how your possible transformation will impact your life and the possibility of others within your family too? This last and final chapter I will discuss the steps I utilized towards **becoming a champion over my life's transformation**. It all started with a vision, a thought and just one single step. The evolution of Veronica Evette Pryor-Faciane was in the hands of Veronica Evette Pryor-Faciane. The things I will share were the steps I utilized that fit my journey. You can learn from these steps and craft your journey to greater and true happiness. Even when Apostle Paul was going through, he thought himself happy.

__I think myself happy__, King Agrippa, because I shall answer for myself this day before thee touching all the things whereof I am accused of the Jews:
~Acts 26:2 (KJV)

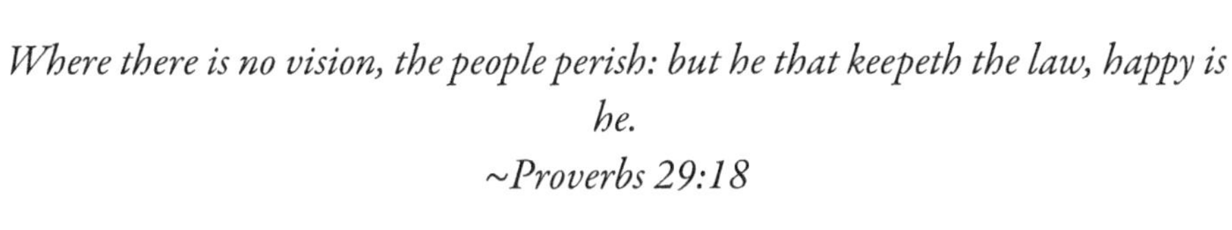

Where there is no vision, the people perish: but he that keepeth the law, happy is he.
~Proverbs 29:18

If you will change, everything will change for you. Don't wait for things to change. Change doesn't start out there, change starts within…. All change starts with you.
~Jim Rohn

I WILL DISCUSS THE steps utilized along my journey towards discovering who Veronica truly is. Remember, I was beaten into who Veronica was. I never really grasped the concept of learning my true self. Do you or have you felt like a robot or slave to your past or current circumstances? Not knowing who and how to please those around you assuming it will give you peace of mind. Not knowing this thought process was detrimental mentally, spiritually and physically. I was afraid of being alone with no one to love me. I finally realized the love I sought was inside of me. Yes, I learned this over time from attending therapy session after therapy session, reading and studying the Bible for myself, studying various morning and evening routines to restructure my beliefs, thoughts, habits, words, actions and overall attitude towards life. I had great determination to change. IT TOOK WORK! I did lots of self-study, reading and listening to audiobook after audiobook (i.e. Wayne Dyer, Tony Robbins, Mel Robbins, Jim Kwik, Oprah Winfrey, Lisa Nichols, Napoleon Hill, Dale Carnegie, Bob Proctor, Joe Dispenza Yuval Noah Harari, Earl Nightingale excreta). From sun-up to sun-down I learned how to be mindful of what I allowed in my system.

Your beliefs become your thoughts,
Your thoughts become your words,
Your words become your actions,

Your actions become your habits,
Your habits become your values,
Your values become your destiny.

~Gandhi

IT WAS TIME FOR ME to start living my blessed life, ya' heard me (in my New Orleans accent). Please remember, it was imperative for me to put in the work daily, whether I felt like it or not. I will not stop investing in learning. Knowledge is only power if I learn and put it into action.

I LEARNED THAT EVEN when I did not believe in the steps, when I did not believe in the affirmations or when I did not see change and the rate I desired (DEEP BREATH). I kept pushing! Will you keep pushing? Do you think you deserve better yet? I know you do! I had to control the thoughts within my mind that expressed an alternative rate and date of completion. I became frustrated when things did not go the way I perceived they would. When going through the process, I learned to look at everything as a blessing even when I was learning a very hard lesson. **Never forget, change is a reaping process. Be mindful of the seeds you are planting.** You must hit it, if you want to get it!!

Do not be deceived: God cannot be mocked. A man reaps what he sows'
~Galatians 6:7

AS IN ANY SPORT, IT requires conditioning of the body and mind. Thus, if you want to be a winner, you must train your brain with the attributes of a winner, not a quitter. Do you currently feel as if you are moving on automatic pilot from day to day? I did! Guess what? You are too! Not being mindful and staying in the present, can lead to anxiety, stress and depression. Trust me I know. I also have a strong feeling that you may have experienced this feeling also. Well, am I correct? It's ok...you will be the only one hearing the answer to all the questions posed within my manuscript.

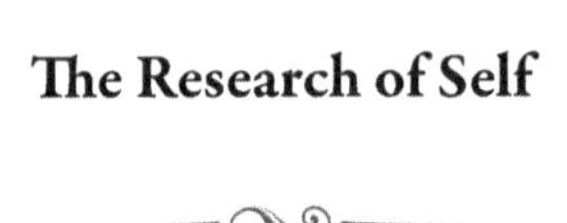

The Research of Self

I HAVE ALWAYS LOVED research, so why not develop my own hypothesis pertaining to what it would take for me to experience positive change and truly live? I did not want my children to carry on any negative traits or generational curses within our bloodline. Will they be perfect? No. God said all have sinned and fallen short of the glory of God. *(Romans 3:23-NIV)*. I was taught in accounting, garbage in equals' garbage out by one of Xavier University of Louisiana accounting professors. Ok, I needed to rid myself of the garbage my parents passed on to me, so, I would not pass it on to my children. Veronica you ask, "Where do you begin?"

The key to change begins with educating yourself, being mindful and applying the knowledge you learn towards cultivating new habits and beliefs. My new favorite saying is:

CONTROL YOUR THOUGHTS daily. Never allow your thoughts to control how you to live your best blessed life. You are "The CEO" of your life. Others should not control the add or subtraction button in Your Life. If they cannot add to your happiness, NEVER ALLOW them to subtract from it.
~Veronica Pryor-Faciane

I ADAPTED THIS BELIEF from my studies about why I felt I could not get out of my trauma. Even though I was no longer physically living in that trauma, I still was reacting and moving in my sleep as if the abuse was still happening to me during my sleep. My husband explained to me how I was fighting, fussing and acting nightly. Now, things are much better. My mind was not free. Even though he was incarcerated physically, I was imprisoned in my mind. This was my mom's challenge too. She expressed continually, how the thoughts would not leave and she was so tired. My mom told me I was strong and I damn sure fought like a beast to rid my body and mind of all the infection and disease placed within me by my birth father's words. I had to identify and reconstruct the self-sabotaging habits and beliefs that were prohibiting from living my best blessed life. Do you have a desire to restructure habits and beliefs that having been leading to not so pleasant places in life? I learned how to slow my decision-making process to reap response and not a reaction. Guess what? This may sound strange, but I feel good evening during challenging times because I have a peace like none other during the mist of the storm. I am in a fixed fight, But God! Well, how bad do you want it? How bad do you want to feel freedom and peace?

TRAUMA VICTIMS OFTEN believe that there is no hope of overcoming. Do you feel this way currently? I have in the past. I used prescribed medicine to help with their emotions which can lead to other issues/addictions. There is nothing wrong with seeking mental health to achieve balance within your life. ***Please do not stop taking your medication without consulting your physician.*** I am currently in a very good place, but it has not always been that way and I feel better than if I had the medicine in my system. REMEMBER.... I am going through my process. Don't just stop your medication. That would not be wise.

Weekly/Outpatient Therapy

THERAPY WAS VERY IMPORTANT towards my transformational foundation resurfacing process. I have learned to feel my feelings no matter what they are and let them pass as a fading thought. No longer holding the thoughts of needing to keep everyone safe was pivotal and monumental in the restructuring of my daily thought process. During outpatient therapy, I learned how to apply this concept to my life's actions which initializes within my thoughts.

Releasing the habit of being a rescuer was imperative in the development of balance within my own life as well. I have heard numerous people make the comment that they don't want to talk to someone who has problems too. This statement is shocking especially since everyone could challenge a primary care doctor, teacher, boss, and teller at the bank, preacher or anyone they don't agree with. It is true that you must be mindful of what you allow in your spirit; however, you can learn from the mistakes and teachings from others.

1 DEAR FRIENDS, DO not believe every spirit, but test the spirits to see whether they are from God, because many false prophets have gone out into the world. 2 This is how you can recognize the Spirit of God: Every spirit that acknowledges that Jesus Christ has come in the flesh is from God, 3 but every spirit that does not acknowledge Jesus is not from God. This is the spirit of the antichrist, which you have heard is coming and even now is already in the world. 4 You, dear children, are from God and have overcome them, because the one who is in you is greater than the one who is in the world. 5 They are from the world and therefore speak from the viewpoint of the world, and the world listens to them. 6 We are from God, and whoever knows God listens to us; but whoever is not from God does not listen to us. This is how we recognize the Spirit of truth and the spirit of falsehood.
~1 John 4: 1-6 (NIV)

YOU CAN FIND EDUCATION from every aspect of life, when you are mindful of your vision. Your application of those teachings is what is key to change. Don't not get me wrong, I still have great empathy and love for all I meet; however, learning about healthy boundaries is key to sustaining balance in daily life. If I receive a since of discomfort, even from a doctor, removing myself from the situation is important to maintaining my life's balancing. For those that have experienced abuse, the feeling of being obligated to the abuser or/and the fear of saying no often leaves a feeling of being in hell with no roadmap out. Often fearing more retaliation or just to tired mentally or physically to care tends to be the mental state of the victim. You deserve better. Trust me, you do. I know I did and I still do.

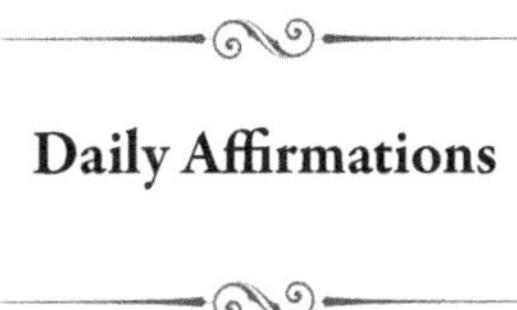

Daily Affirmations

HAVE YOU HEARD OF A teacher redirecting student with hopes of achieving a specific goal or goals? Implementing the use of affirmations was key to my metamorphosis. No one could ignite and continue my mindfulness learning processes but me. Serving as teacher at times and a student all the time was imperative. I learned how powerful affirmations are. What are affirmations? I am so glad you ask. They are positive, powerful and impactful statements that are repeated daily. Repeating the statements is a form of redirecting and inspiring the programs within the mind on a subconscious level. The power of "I Am" was key in manifesting, motivating and triggering my mind to move in a positive direction.

OKAY, LET'S BE HONEST, I tried this, but I did not actually see it working for some time. However, I did not stop my daily practice. I look forward to my affirmations now as part of my morning and evening routines. Often people's thoughts tend to gravitate towards negative statements surrounding life's events and situations. Okay, have you notice when you say or think that something isn't going to work or fail, it normally does. Choose words that build up thought process and not tear it down.

YOUR SUBCONSCIOUS MIND will start to accept the statements as true and replace conflicting ones the more you keep saying them. My fellow sisters or brothers utilize my truths to encourage you towards pressing on and living your truth. I no longer require validation from others and one day neither will you. Now, don't get me wrong, I love the right attention from my King David. Restructuring my life/mind was up to me and I am LOVING THE REFLECTION IN THE MIRROR. I no longer say I don't love the skin I am in. I am in Love with Me ...... (deep breath)...Feeling Refreshed. I did this habit until the habit now does me as John Assaraf spoke about. No longer allowing my emotions to disempower but empower me. I believe your attitude determines your altitude thus, why should I allow other people's opinions of me be more important than my own?

The people who get the most approval in life, are the ones who care less about it and the ones that get the least approval are the one going after it.
~Dr. Wayne Dyer

GOING TO THE NEXT LEVEL in life required me to sharpen my focus and continuing to push through no matter what. I viewed my setbacks as setups for my grater. How do you choose to look at your setbacks? I don't FEAR (false evidence appearing real) the challenges of life anymore. I noticed my fear subsided when I did not allow the thoughts to run around in my head, once again, as bad little kids with no home training. I keep in the forefront of my mind, I am in a fixed fight. But, I do play a major roll along this journey. Choosing to discontinue my self-defeating attitude was a radical step along my life's journey. I utilized Mel Robbins' five second rule to control feelings of anger, impatience, frustration, and fear. I noticed it took a bit longer for me to restructure my thoughts pertaining to disappointment and sadness. I am a work in process. (lol)

MY AFFIRMATIONS WERE created by first, making a conscious effort to identify and journal my negative belief system and self-talk. Second, the negative beliefs within me were turned into positive affirmations. My thought process that was once dysfunctioning is now being crafted into a proper positive functioning thoughts process, allowing me to create my best blessed life.

BELOW ARE A FEW EXAMPLES *of my daily affirmations: (spoken in a believable affirming but gentle manner- you don't want to sound like you are mad at self)*

- I am enough.

- I love my life.

- This too shall pass.

- I am in control of my thoughts, feelings and beliefs.

- I am bold, beautiful and blessed.

- I am in control of my health and happiness.

- I learn positive things from all of my life's experiences.

- I am living my perfect truth and balance in this moment.

- I am a grateful hearted person.

- Life is happing for me and not to me.

- I am a warrior and not a worrier.

- I love and accept myself for who I am.

- I am the creator of my life's balance.

- I am mindful and restructure beliefs that condition meanings that cause stress.

- I believe in my skills and abilities to love myself unconditionally.

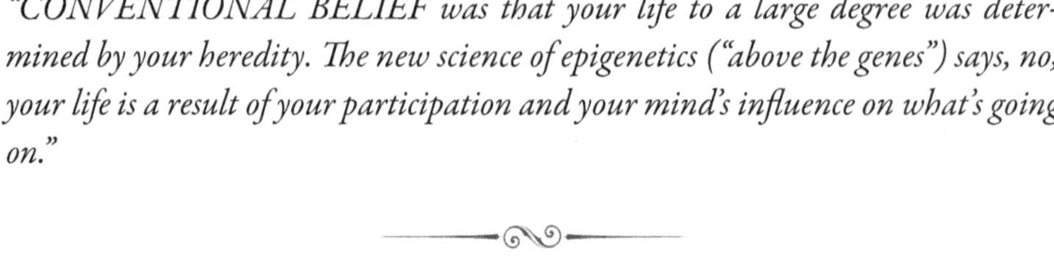

"CONVENTIONAL BELIEF was that your life to a large degree was determined by your heredity. The new science of epigenetics ("above the genes") says, no, your life is a result of your participation and your mind's influence on what's going on."

~Bruce Lipton

Mindfulness

MINDFULNESS ACCORDING the Merriam-Webster's Dictionary is the practice of maintaining a nonjudgmental state of heightened or complete awareness of one's thoughts, emotions, or experiences on a moment- to-moment basis." I have learned, over time to be aware of my internal and external "present" state of being. Mindfulness allowed me to be consciously aware and respond accordingly. It is a feeling that has me in a peaceful state of being, almost all the time. Yes, even when with the necked eye, it appears as if my world is crumbling down. Learning to connect with the spirit man/woman is key. I feel a peace that surpasses all understanding, as discussed in the Bible. It feels so good to have a different vision about life. I don't dwell on the past nor do I allow my thoughts to fast-forward to the future in a non-productive manner (anxiety). During my mindfulness studies, I become more aware of the core beliefs instilled in me from family and society. This revelation was monumental during the mindfulness implementation process. Becoming aware of those beliefs that I should keep and those that needed to be deleted for me to grow spiritually.

I HAVE LEARNED HOW to enjoy my children, husband and life by being mentally in the present. (slow deep breath—-ummmmm) I Thank God. Stopping to smell the roses has a new and profound meaning to me now. I am not saying that issues or challenges in life don't shake me, but they no longer break me. Yes, my children are being a challenge in school and daily life, but I know it is a spiritual warfare. Yes, I am currently having financial challenges...spiritual warfare. Yes, couples don't always agree and I experience challenges in our relationship. spiritual warfare. The list can go on and on. I stop, feel my feelings, whether it is sadness, anger, happiness or joy. I no longer react but respond to those feelings. Being in the present allows my responses to be more controlled and positive. When life gives me lemons, I have learned to make sweet delicious lemonade. I try to see the good or the lesson I should grasp from every situation. (Smiling with Gratitude) Individuals can learn how to regulate themselves and receive balance in life. The benefits of mindfulness are (PositivePsychologyProgram.Com, 2017):

- Well-being is promoted by being mindful of your emotions and thoughts. Being self-aware allows for a reduction in stress, anxiety and developing various sicknesses.
- Being mindful helps your working memory.
- Mindfulness helps to suppress depressive symptoms.
- Mindfulness helps in the utilization of an individual's personal strengths (i.e. compassion and wisdom). Mindfulness allows for neuroplasticity (structural and functional) changes of the brain, thus allowing for self-regulation and compassion to build our brain function in a positive manner.
- Mindfulness practice raises the mood of happiness activity in the left prefrontal cortex. When a person is depressed or anxious, the activity is higher on the left prefrontal cortex.
- Mindfulness allows individuals to become more maladaptive to setbacks or trials and helps you make better decisions.
- Mindfulness allows for the amygdala (the stress-area of the brain) to be reduced thus changing how people respond to stressful situations increased the overall wellbeing (physical and mental) of an individual.

Mindfulness was one of the factors in my transformation. I went to outpatient/inpatient therapy, group therapy, individual therapy, see a psychiatrist and hypnotherapy. I was determined to change and gain control of my thoughts. I was tired of having the negative internal conversations that were not serving me in a positive manner. In my opinion, my belief system/faith had to be strengthened by becoming mindful/aware of the negative beliefs that were not serving me along my transformational journey. Are you ready for change? Are you tired of just existing on a day to day basis? Are you sick and tired of being sick and tired with no direction? Do not continue in your flustered state of being. Assistance and direction will be given later towards the end of this chapter. My mission is to assist and serve as a guide for others seeking positive transformation. I had to become mindful of my habits achieve the change I desired. As important as this is in my opinion, it was not taught in my home nor did I learn it in school.

Habits

I LEARNED THAT MY LIFE'S habits and beliefs damaged my thought process, which caused a great imbalance, spiritually, physically and emotionally. Once again, I was mindful of the beliefs from family and society that I needed to keep and delete for my continued mental, physical and spiritual growth. In the book, The Power of Habit by Charles Duhigg, (2014) it was noted:

1. Individuals spend have of the time they are woke doing automatic behaviors. A study done in 2006 at Duke University found that 45% of our daily behaviors are automatic.
2. Your brain saves energy processing automatic habits. It is like the central processing system of the body utilizing 25% of the oxygen in the body.
3. Habits can be a challenge to break due the structure of the brain. Understanding the complexities would require more research.
4. Having some sort of spiritual belief/faith help individuals to change

habits. For example, the 12 steps used with AA helps with sobriety.

Sounds like what the Bible talks about faith without works is dead. They choose to live a better life passed their challenge with alcohol by believing and working towards changing. This concept can be applied to all areas of your life don't you think?

1. Mr. Duhigg also spoke on how one keystone habit can start positive changes in other areas of an individual's life.

A habit is defined by Merriam-Webster's dictionary as an acquired behavior pattern regularly followed until it has become almost involuntary like anxiety, depression and stress in my opinion. I was affected by these three partners in crime, but I was committed to hiring and firing things and people that were not serving in a positive emotional state. Now, do not think this process was easy. Remember, I had to do become the CEO (Chief Executive Officer) of my own life. Yes, I was scared, uncertain, and sometimes (a lot of times) wanted to just quit. Then, I thought of my why, at the time. Did I want my future (my children) to experience the lack of mental direction and clarity I had? Did I want them to do just enough to exist and not truly live? Did I want them to just get stuff but never experience true wealth? You can have all the money in the world and never have wealth in my opinion. You cannot have all the money and do experience wealth when your mind is free.

My subconscious mind had to be revamped/reprogramed. I **had to release** not lose the beliefs and habits that lead to my stinking thinking thoughts. Now, I want to bring to your attention I utilized the word **RELEASE.** I had no desire to pick-up/revisit those things that were harming to my greater. In life when you lose keys are something else of value, you look for the item. I WAS NOT GOING BACK.

Do a habit until the habit does you.

~John Assaraf

—⟋⟍⟍◯—

I learned how to utilize my body and controlling my thoughts (to help calm me when I feel my left prefrontal cortex (depression, anxiety and stress) jumping into the driver's seat of my emotions. I learned how to control my breathing patterns to calm the circuits in my brain. (Deep Breath...) I am dealing with life with great poise and elegance in my opinion. It feels good when others attempted to shake me, yet I forge onward standing strong and calm. Thank you, God! Of course, I had those remember when people. Those who remember when I was not at my best. You will experience this also but keep pushing. After a while, they will ask you how you changed, thus becoming the change you desire to see in the world. Change begins with a single step.

—⟋⟍⟍◯—

"If you can't fly, then run,
if you can't run, then walk,
if you can't walk, then crawl,
but whatever you do,
you have to keep moving forward."

~Rev. Dr. Martin Luther King Jr.

—⟋⟍⟍◯—

Developing Self-Love

—⟋⟍⟍◯—

I BECAME SICK AND TIRED of being sick and tired, my "Why" shifted for my transformational process to continue. My love for my children and my husband only took me only so far. I did not have true love for myself. How could

I love them like they desired to be loved if I did not know how to love myself first?

OKAY, ON TO THE NEXT phase. I continued individual therapy and started researching other habits I could implement towards MY Greater. I added a daily practice of morning and evening affirmations, gratitude, meditation and prayer. Consistency was KEY in those actions taking positive roots within my life. If you decide to continue this journey, follow the link that will be found at the end of manuscript to sign-up and receive FREE MATERIAL that will assist you to begin your transformational process, ending the generational curses, acceptance patterns of abuse/trauma and other challenges that have been blocking you from becoming and living your best life due to faulty mental thoughts and programing. Remember how impressionable children are. How was your youth? What type of environment where you exposed to?

EVERYTHING STEMS FROM a thought good or bad. I am grateful beyond measure for becoming a no limit adult with dreams, aspirations and an imagination again. Remember pretending as a little child and the joy that came from it. Pretending is nothing more than establishing goals and dreams. Why have the attitude that because you are a certain age, you can not change the trajectory of your life? It is up to you to stop feeling and speaking over your life as is there is no hope for happiness. I am 48 years old as of January 2019, I am choosing to do what makes Veronica happy and it feels GREAT (in my Tony the Tiger Voice). What I choose to visualize can materialize, when I work for it. I began altering my speech daily. By this I did not speak negative things into the atmosphere/universe. Now, did thoughts come? Of course, I choose to not give continual life to the thoughts that I knew were not serving me in a positive manner. A life that planted continual seeds of depression, anxiety and stress. I was tired of living an adverse life. How about you? Aren't you tired of just existing from day to day or speaking havoc and death into your life? I was. This is why I made the decision to change for self and not just my family.

1. A man shall eat good by the fruit of his mouth: but the soul of the transgressors shall eat violence. 3. He that keepeth his mouth keepeth his life: but he that openeth wide his lips shall have destruction.

~Proverbs 13:2-3(KJV)

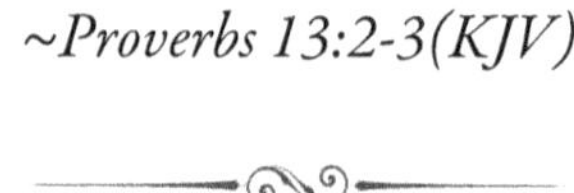

I made a conscious decision to accomplish my dreams no matter what. I made a conscious decision to be mindful what come out of my mouth. Is it a challenge? Yes! Do I have days that I think about throwing in the towel? Yes! Do I wonder what steps I should take to accomplish my dreams of becoming a renowned author, transformational speaker and coach? Daily...failure is not an option. I want to help our youth, though mindfulness training, develop into stronger mental adults. I desire to help any adult seeking mental peace and clarity within their daily paths of life. It is an important part of my mission to share what I have learned with others. My life is continually moving onward to better. I see my children evolving in a positive manner, due to changes I have made. I see how my relationship with my husband is changing due to changes I made within me. I can see my blended family becoming stronger due to changes I made within me. Do you see that pattern? Everything begins with self. Stop trying to focus on others and focus on self. When I stop trying to "fix or get someone to behave the way I assumed they should" and FOCUSED ON VERONICA, my entire environment shifted towards greater. Thank you for taking this time to learn and hopeful apply phases of my life's journey towards becoming your best self. Remember, to create a personal roadmap for your journey.

In conclusion, I just want to say Thank You and express how Grateful Beyond Measure I am for you taking your precious time to read about my journey. It is my hope that you will begin, if you have not already, the steps towards developing into your best and true self. I am here to assist during this process for those desiring assistance.

I am also in the process of creating a private interactive Facebook group for those who are developing their **New** true **ID**.

Jesus modeled how transformation should appear, no matter how humble your beginnings were. Remember the question posed by Nathanael, "Can any good thing come out of Nazareth?" (John 1:46) (BibleOdyssey.org, 2019). We always hear, if they talked about Jesus, what about you? However, have you really taken the time to meditate on this statement? The roadmap to life was established by studies in the Bible along with reading the book of the way by Tao Te Ching and others. The overall teachings are based on the belief that sustainer of all life (God for me) is omnipotent and cannot truly be explained with human terminology because God is ALL PERFECT.

Never allow people's view of where you come from or your view of looking down on self, dictate where you are going. Nathanael criticized Jesus because he was not from the Judean elite part of society. Does that sound like what goes on today? But God! There are those that look down on people that come from areas where the population is working poor. There are those that desire to improve themselves; however, they cannot truly become their best due to negative impact on certain core values imbedded within their foundation.

Just because someone has more financial means, it does not mean they have a stronger mental positive state of being. Nathanael felt that God could not have sent Jesus to Nazareth. Philip's claim had to be wrong. The savior came from where? Nazareth...lol yes, He did. Jesus led by example how when being tried by the devil in the wilderness.... He pressed on as we must do also. No matter what challenge comes your way, remember it is either a blessing or a lesson. In my opinion a lesson is a blessing too! Always ignore the, I remember when crew. Apparently, they forgot about the skeletons that are still hanging in their closets. God said Alll have sinned so, that means no one is excluded. It's all about having balance. Always Remember:

*When there is **no enemy within**, the enemies outside cannot hurt you.*

~African Proverb

Do not be your own worst enemy mentally. For those having the desire to develop the methodology that best enables them to change the negative core beliefs, I challenge you to try this 30-day Gratitude Challenge to begin your journey. There is scientific proof concerning the positive affects received from being grateful/thankful. I have experience exponential growth in proportion to the work that I have placed into my transformational process. Never forget garbage in garbage out......watch what you allow into your spiritual, physical, and mental life. You are the CEO of your happiness and gratitude constitutes what you are happy for. Fire and hire as needed from any of those three areas of your life to maintain balance. I realize that I Matter, you matter, WE ALL MATTER.

Upon reading, it was noted in an article written by Morin, A., (2015), that there are 7 scientifically proven benefits of gratitude:

1. When you show yourself friendly, you open the door to ongoing relationships with others. It is important to just say "Thank You." I have experience more and more doors opening for me. I cannot explain how pavers are being lad for my success and current transformation, they just are. For that, I am Grateful Beyond Measure.

2. Individuals develop a greater since of empathy. When I empathize with others I notice my aggression levels decreased. I was not as angry. The article notes how one behaves in a prosocial manner no matter if the actions are not reciprocated. I explained to my husband, I don't have the desire to get back at others that have wronged me. I know that Karma works. Why should I shake my balance because of their actions? I experienced being questioned concerning things I am

currently doing. I did not get mad nor upset. God's vision for me is not for others to see and it is ok. I am at peace with people passing their thoughts, because I am no longer a people pleaser. I love helping and I no longer feel I must rescue the world. Realizing that you can give information; however, it is up to the individual to utilize the knowledge to grow or be stagnant. For that, I am Grateful Beyond Measure.

3. Gratitude has improved my physical health tremendously. Research has shown that that those who express gratitude have, fewer aches and pains. Boy oh boy is that true. I missed more time from work because of ailments (physical and mental). Your body develops diseases when you are not at ease/peace. Individuals that are grateful tend to keep up with wellness visits and their overall health.

Hint: Gratitude aligns with mindfulness. By being grateful, you will become mindful things no matter how big or small events occur within your life on a daily basis. Thus, cultivating a positive light that enhances greater mental clarity and physical health. For that, I am Grateful Beyond Measure.

1. There is great psychological improvement when gratitude is implemented within an individual's daily life by reducing toxic emotions. One of the leading gratitude researchers, Mr. Robert Emmons, research confirms that gratitude reduces depression. Yessss Mr. Emmons, my depression is under control. I do not have those days where I feel that I am continually sinking into a black hole. Days were it hurts just to get out of bed with no desire to eat. Days where my get up and go was nooooo where around. Now, despite challenges, I can always find something to be grateful for, thus thrusting me to a new level of happiness. For that, I am Grateful Beyond Measure.

2. Self-Esteem is improved with gratitude. Based on various studies, social comparisons are reduced, and individuals applaud each other's accomplishments. I have learned to not allow others perception of where they think I should be, affect my joy and peace. Pleasing of self...yes.... People-pleasing... Deleted. This is one of the ways I was able

to move past what people think and write my story for God's glory. For that, I am Grateful Beyond Measure.

3. With gratitude I sleep better. This is one of the reasons the challenge encompasses journaling to send more energy into your gratitude journey towards becoming your true selves. I no longer need sleep aids to turn off the negative and fast paced thoughts. Tossing and turning no more. Waking up before the alarm clock. (Deep Breath) For that, I am Grateful Beyond Measure.

4. Mental strength is increased with gratitude. As in any area of life, the more you practice the stronger you become. A study was done on veterans from the Vietnam War. Those who utilize gratitude daily, have lower rates of PTSD (Post Traumatic Stress Disorder). Yes, once again, I have experience this too. Remember, those who experienced this level of abuse as I did, also suffer from PTSD. My episodes/triggers are more under controlled than ever before. Cognitive Behavioral Therapy, Hypnotherapy, Neuro-Linguistic Programming Therapy, excetera helped me with my dissociative defenses, spacing out along with memory disturbances. I believe this contributed to my ADHD. Now I am doing so much better and for that, I am Grateful Beyond Measure.

Rejoice always, pray continually, give thanks in all circumstances; for this is the will of God in Christ Jesus for you.
1 Thessalonians 5:16-18 (NIV)

As we express our gratitude, we must never forget that the highest appreciation is not to utter words, but to live by them.
~John F. Kennedy

Gratitude unlocks the fullness of life. It turns what we have into enough, and more. It turns denial into acceptance, chaos to order, confusion to clarity. It can turn a meal into a feast, a house into a home, a stranger into a friend.
~Melody Beattie

30 Day Gratitude Challenge

<u>Morning & Night</u>

I challenge you to wake-up for the next 30 days and journal/say at least 3 things you are grateful for as soon as your eyes open that are not related to materialistic items (i.e. I am grateful for being alive another day, I am grateful for having a restful night, I am grateful for the positive changes that are coming in my life etc.) Have a notebook, journal or voice memo app of some sort to record what you decided to speak on each morning. This form of positive psychology helps with the increasing of an individual's overall well-being. This time is important to all who desire to have control of their day. When saying thank you or I appreciate you, it helps to develop the changes for your greater, just continue being mindful and acknowledge others. This sign of gratitude shows the other individual that they are not being taken for granted. Remember change begins with a single step.

Best Wishes on Your Journey

I Thank You

I want to thank each one for their precious time and attention. It is my hope that you were able to learn from my life's strategies pertaining to overcoming the traumas of daily life. I ask that as you learn and become stronger please pass along the knowledge that you gain. We must be the change we desire to see within the world. We all have experienced some sort to trauma, mine was initiated by the hands of my birth-father. Sexual, mental, physical, spiritual, financial abuse along with incest were the traumas I faced. Your traumas could have been similar or very different. However, hurt still hurts the victim. Generational issues/curses linger when people choose to ignore them. Ignoring an issue does not eliminate it. When you allow that seed to be planted, the root only grows deeper and deeper and continues to strengthen and the families' name decays.

I choose to start chopping at the root of this sort of trauma within my families' lineage. Remember, a fire begins with a single spark. What type of spark or you admitting into the universe? Families often choose to hide or sweep issues within the family under a rug, only hoping to look good for society and in the eyes of those within their community. There are adults that even get mad at those for bringing certain issues to a head within the family. I have spoken with some victims that were blamed by adults for speaking up. BUT GOD! God knows and sees all.

In my opinion, having the Vision of a Champion is what is important in carrying on positivity from generation to generation. One of my younger cousin's (T.J. Pryer) came up with a business with this very slogan for him and one of our cousins', who has transitioned to heaven via the decision of someone who choose to drink and drive, while he was in route to work before T.J could present the dream to Jermaine Pryer (PRYME). It was their dream to play baseball and T.J. had the vision of continuing this dream with the start of the company Visions of Champions. That in my opinion is the beginning of starting generational wealth within a family. Many of my cousins are choosing to change the trajectory of the past. So, what seed are you choosing to plant within your family? Remember, Your Best is Yet to Come when you become mindful of the steps you make along this journey called life.

"Some people will like you. Some people won't like you. So, what. Do not let the opinions of others dictate how you feel about yourself. You, ad you alone dictate your worth. Always believe in yourself. You be the one that dictates what people think of you and how people treat you. Become a believer..... in yourself."

~Joseph Andrus

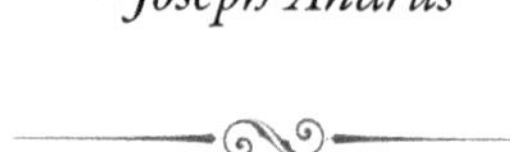

Free Gift

Towards Your Daily Life's Peace & Happiness

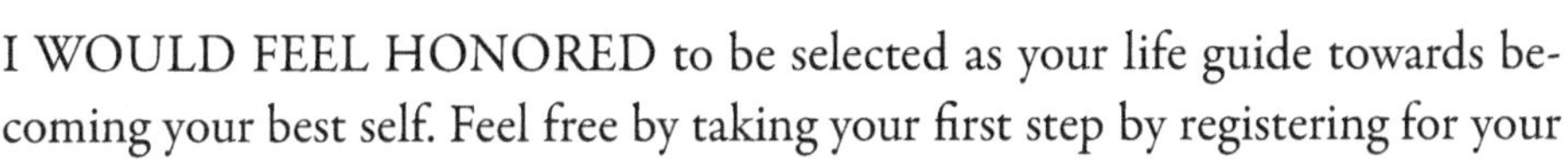

I WOULD FEEL HONORED to be selected as your life guide towards becoming your best self. Feel free by taking your first step by registering for your **"FREE"** 30-minute coaching call towards developing your personal roadmap.
($125.00-Value)
(Vibrational Value- Priceless)

✓ For those who desire how to restructure negative thoughts into positive ones thus, elevating your daily vibration/energy in a positive manner.

✓ For those who want to learn how to show themselves true self-love and rise above their traumas.

✓ For those who want to experience mental clarity and peace from a simple conversation.

✓ For those who want to learn how to develop methods of going through life's challenges instead of allowing them continuously to control the individual.

✓ For those who want to control your anxiety, stress and depression thus, elevating your health and balance daily.

✓ For those who want to control your mornings and evenings to begin and end your day with peace.

✓ For those who want to minimize or end their use of various vices to numb their emotions.

✓ For those who want to live your best life and not go through life just existing.

IF CHOOSE AND ARE COMMITTED work towards greater and becoming your Best Blessed Life by continuing our journey together, please go to WWW.NewIDLifeCoaching.Com[1] to schedule our initial session. Thank you for allowing me to become your life-guide towards greater.

---

1. http://WWW.NewIDLifeCoaching.Com

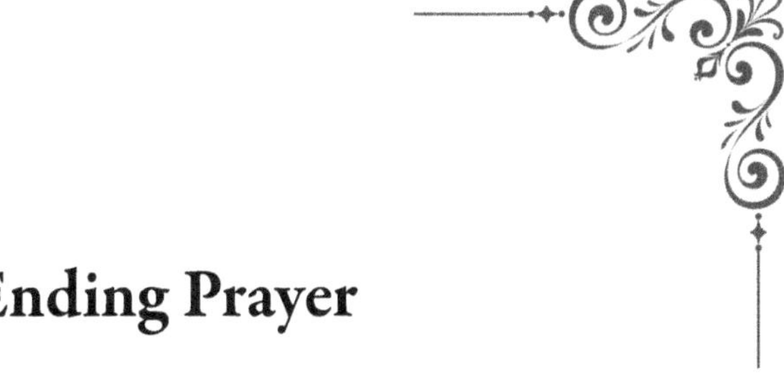

Ending Prayer

LORD, WHATEVER WE FACE today, we can handle it by placing all our cares at your feet. For YOU are The Author and Finisher of our faith. You are The One who restructures, reestablishes and restores. YOU are the one who helped me to move from being (just existing) to becoming (transforming into a diamond). Becoming the precious jewel, one to nurture, one to lead others who have experienced hurt and anguish from individuals they placed their trust and love in. You are the one who will place true self-love into those that seek Your Guidance and eternal peace. The love that will give them the peace that surpasses all understanding. With this belief, individuals can resolve to evolve and transform into the shining diamond that you have predestined them to be. Being shaped, molded and formed into strong minded individuals. Yes, they may bend...but, never will they break. Yes, it takes pressure to make a diamond and I Thank You in The Mighty Name of Jesus for Giving Me the Ability to Withstand the Pressure. I pray that my fellow brother or sister reading this prayer, will continue to press towards the mark of their higher calling.

YOU HAVE RESTRUCTURED my life's infrastructures, and I Thank You! When I thought you had forgotten about me I now can see, that this journey is what has allowed me to become ME and learn my true New ID. So, with humbleness and grace, I now can wear a grateful smile on my face, ever moving towards having an attitude of continual gratitude. I pray this book serves as a guide, impacting others in a positive manner. Learning to give them this day their daily bread (staying in the present) and dealing with tomorrow when it comes just like The Our Father's Prayer states, "Give us this day our daily bread."

(Matthew 6:11 - NIV). Thus, releasing worry, stress, depression and anxiety in The Mighty Name of Jesus Amen, Amen, and Amen.

Veronica Pryor-Faciane
I Speak My Truth.... What about you?

References

AMERICAN ACADEMY OF Pediatrics (2012). The Lifelong Effects of Early Childhood Adversity and

Toxic Stress. *American Academy of Pediatrics.* January 2012; Volume 129/Issue 1. Retrieved from http://pediatrics.aappublications.org/content/129/1/e232

doi: 10.1542/peds.2011-2663[1]
Australian Government Australian Institute of Family Studies. (January 2013). The long-term

effects of child sexual abuse, CFCA Paper No. 11. *Australian Institute of Family Studies.*

Retrieved from https://aifs.gov.au/cfca/publications/long-term-effects-child-sexual-abuse/impact-child-sexual-abuse-mental-health).

Bible Gateway, (2018). Retrieved From https://www.biblegateway.com
Duhigg, Charles. (2014). The Power of Habit: Why we do what we do in life and business. New York: Random House.
Keep Kids Safe, (2018). 6 Ways Molestation Affects Adult Survivors.

Keepkidssafe.org. Retrieved from http://keepkidssafe.org/6-ways-molestation-affects-adult-survivors/

Harden, Lauren, (2014). Depression Treatment: Inpatient vs. Outpatient. *Healthy Place.*

Retrieved from https://www.healtyplace.com/blogs/mentlhealthtreatmentcircle/2014/ 02/depression-[2]treatment-outpatient-inpatient

---

1.   https://doi.org/10.1542/peds.2011-2663

2. https://www.healtyplace.com/blogs/mentalhealthtreatmentcircle/2014/02/depression-

Health Line, (n.d.). The Effects of Depression in Your Body. *Health Line.* Retrieved from https://www.healthline.com/health/depression/effects-on-body#1[3]

Kenner, C. S., (2019). Can Anything Good Come Out of Nazareth? (John 1:46). *Bible Odyssey.*

Retrieved from http://www.bibleodyssey.org/places/related-articles/can-anything-good-come-out-of-nazareth.aspx

Living Well, (n.d). Dealing with Anger. *Living Well.* Retrieved from https://www.livingwell.org.au/managing-difficulties/dealing-with-anger/

Morin, A., (2015). 7 Scientifically Proven Benefits of Gratitude. *Psychology Today.* Retrieved

from https://www.psychologytoday.com/us/blog/what-mentally-strong-people-dont-do/201504/7-scientifically-proven-benefits-gratitude

Philosophy News (2011). Talk About Love. Philosophy News. Retrieved from https://www.philosophynews.com/post/2011/06/27/Talk-About-Love.aspx

Positive Psychology Program, (2017). Benefits of Mindfulness. Positive Psychology Program.

Retrieved From https://positivepsychologyprogram.com/mindfulness-positive-psychology-3-great-insights/

PsychCentral,(n.d). Understanding the Effects of Domestic Violence. *PsychCentral.* Retrieved

from https://psychcentral.com/lib/understanding-the-effects-of-domestic-violence/

Psychology Today, (2018). Child Abuse. *Psychology Today.* Retrieved from https://www.psychologytoday.com/us/conditions/child-abuse

"Sexual Abuse of Children." American Academy of Experts in Traumatic Stress. AAETS, n.d.

Retrieved from http://www.aaets.org/article124.htm

SmashMirrors, (2015). The Abuse Cycle. Smash Mirrors. Retrieved from

https://smashedmirrors.wordpress.com/2015/06/23/cycle-of-violence-and-the-honeymoon-phase/

White Ribbon, (2019). What is Domestic Violence. *White Ribbon.* Retrieved from

https://www.whiteribbon.org.au/understand-domestic-violence/what-is-domestic-violence/cycle-of-violence/

---

3.   https://www.healthline.com/health/depression/effects-on-body#a5c02393e59c943d6a75a9241140faca31

About the Author

VERONICA PRYOR-FACIANE is a captivating storyteller that utilizes her journey as a teaching tool to inspire and motivate others desiring to become their *"Best Selves"*. She received her Master's Degree in Psychology with a Concentration in Life Coaching in November 2018. She is the CEO/Founder of New ID (a/k/a Inspirational Diamonds) Life Coaching LLC. Veronica classifies her craft within the genres of Transformation Speaker/ Life Coach and Author. Her mission is to assist as a guide for those that have experienced trauma, including survivors of domestic violence, incest, early childhood abuse, sexual assault along with other life challenges to develop a successful roadmap towards their NEW ID and not the identification that was given to them by their parents, environment or various negative societal factors. This passion was invoked after developing a warrior and not worrier mindset, overcoming 28 years of incest, financial, physical, spiritual and domestic violence suffered at the hands of her birthfather.

Before the inception of New ID Life Coaching, Veronica served as an auditor with a major school system for over 17 years in the Baton Rouge, serving as a financial literacy trainer for aspiring principals as well as training secretaries and principal's concerning the proper handling of school funds throughout the district. She has worked with youth and adults in varying capacities since 1983 to present (camp assistant, volunteering through various organizations as Key Club, Student Council and NABA (National Association of Black Accounts) of Xavier University just to name a few. Veronica has always strived for excellence despite life's adversities by accomplishing the following:

- Graduating from Xavier University of New Orleans with honors in

1994, President of Xavier University's National Association of Black Accountants, member of Alpha Kappa Mu Honor Society, a member of Who's Who Among Students, selected to participate in a Graduate Internship during my junior year of collage at Notre Dame University, and other academic distinctions.

HER MISSION HAS ALWAYS been too worked in various facets within God's Kingdom (i.e. teach during Vacation Bible School several years, directing choirs and planning events such as a Back to School Rally. She is an enlightened and transparent individual utilizing the skill-sets acquired throughout her life's journey as guide to assist others towards living their Best Lives. She is a living example of how restructuring negative thoughts via mindfulness can pave the way to living your best life. She often reminds others that:

Mottos to live by from Veronica Pryor-Faciane, MA

***A Positive Mindset is key towards evolving into the precious gem "YOU DESIRE TO BE."

***NEVER ALLOW YOUR THOUGHTS to control you. You control your thoughts throughout the day.

***It takes pressure to make a diamond, thus develop the mindset to craft life's coals into precious diamonds by:

D-etermined to developing an

I – nnovative & inspirational

A -lternative

M- indset leading

O- nward to a

N-ew positive

D-irection

<u>Social Media and Email Contact Information</u>

NewIDLifeCoaching888@gmail.com

New ID with Veronica Pryor-Faciane

NewID888

Don't miss out!

Visit the website below and you can sign up to receive emails whenever Veronica Pryor-Faciane publishes a new book. There's no charge and no obligation.

https://books2read.com/r/B-A-TRWH-HSYX

BOOKS 2 READ

Connecting independent readers to independent writers.